50 CUTE ANIMALS
COLLORING BOOK FOR KIDS

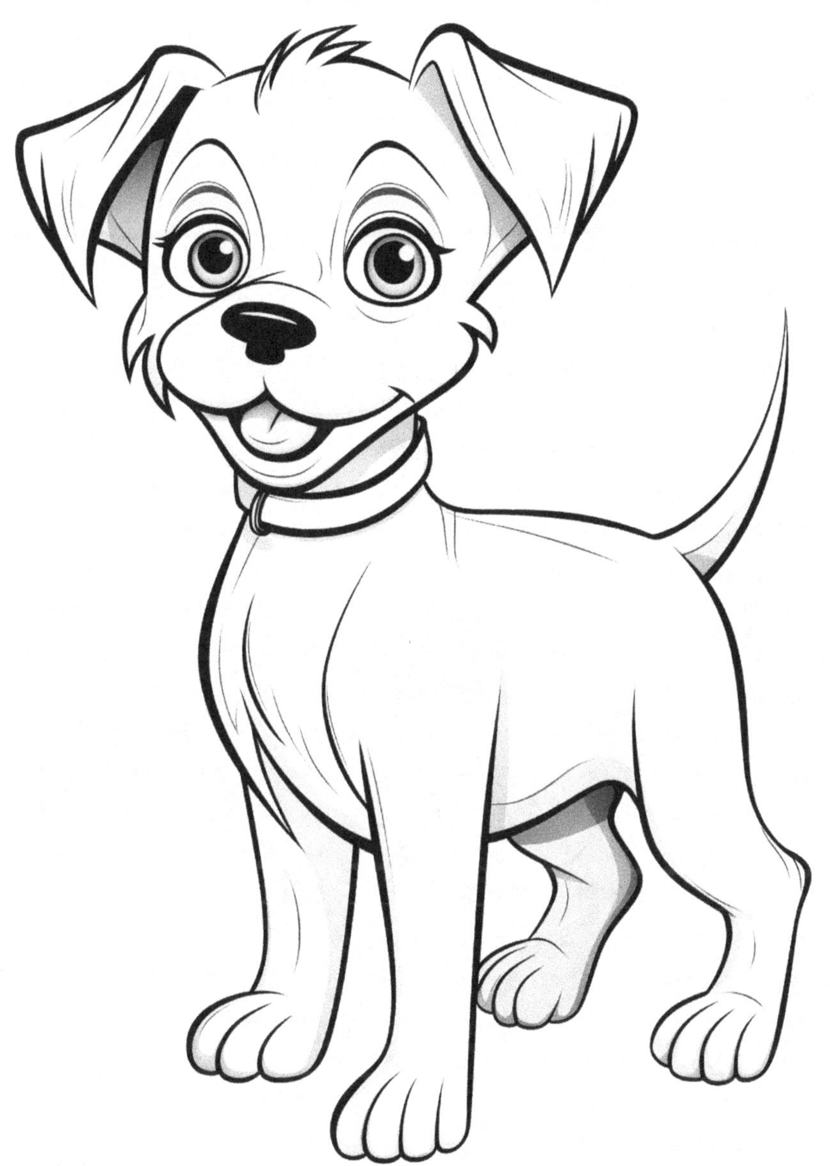

Instagram: ovi_books

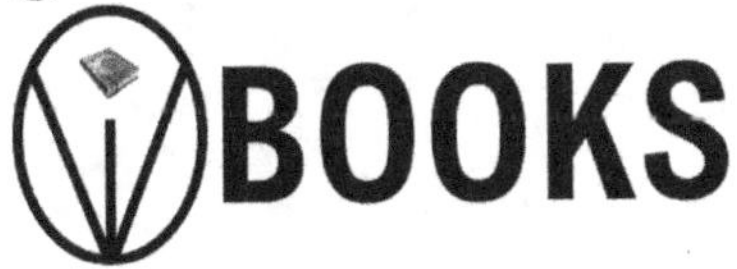
BOOKS

This book belongs to:

____

____

____

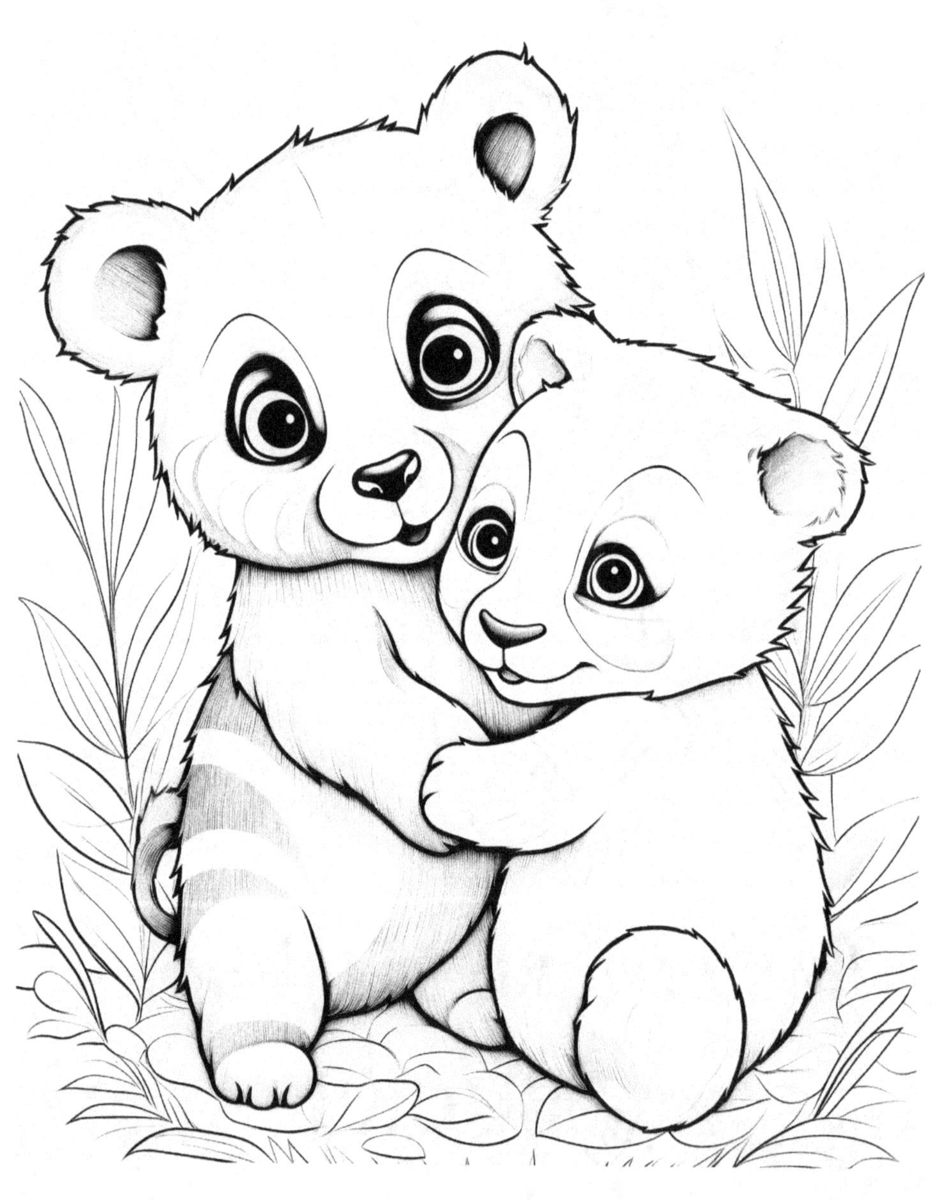

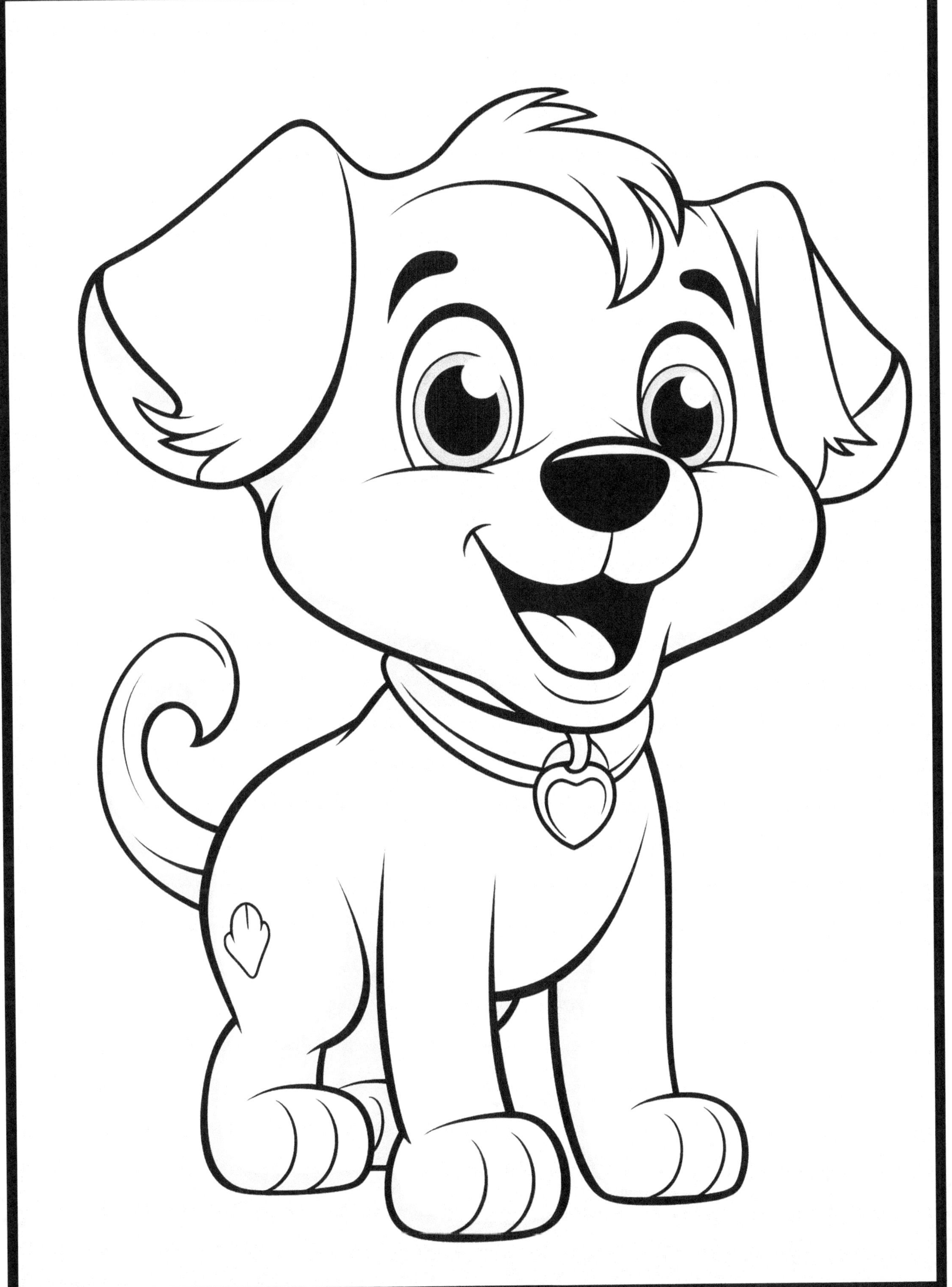

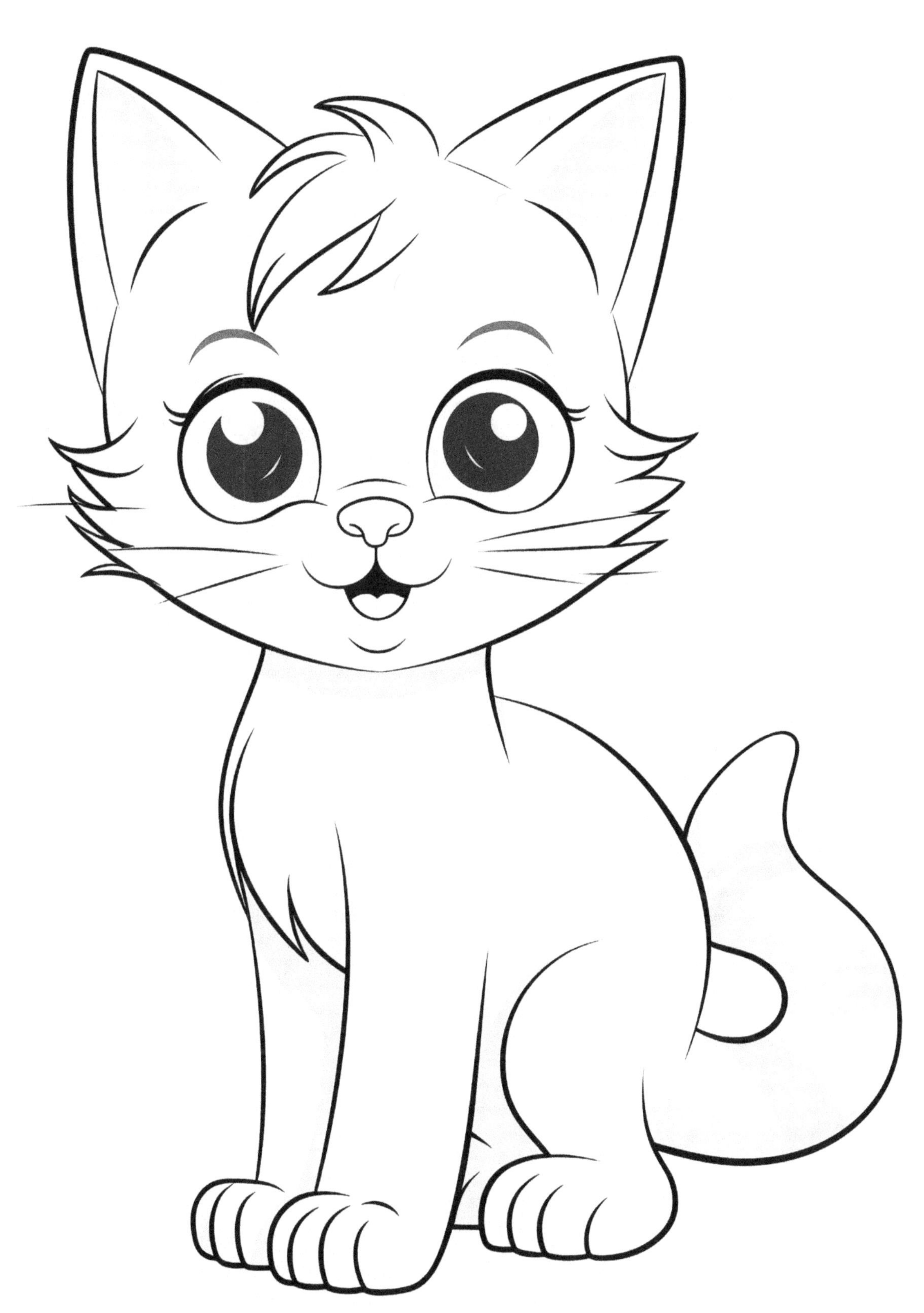

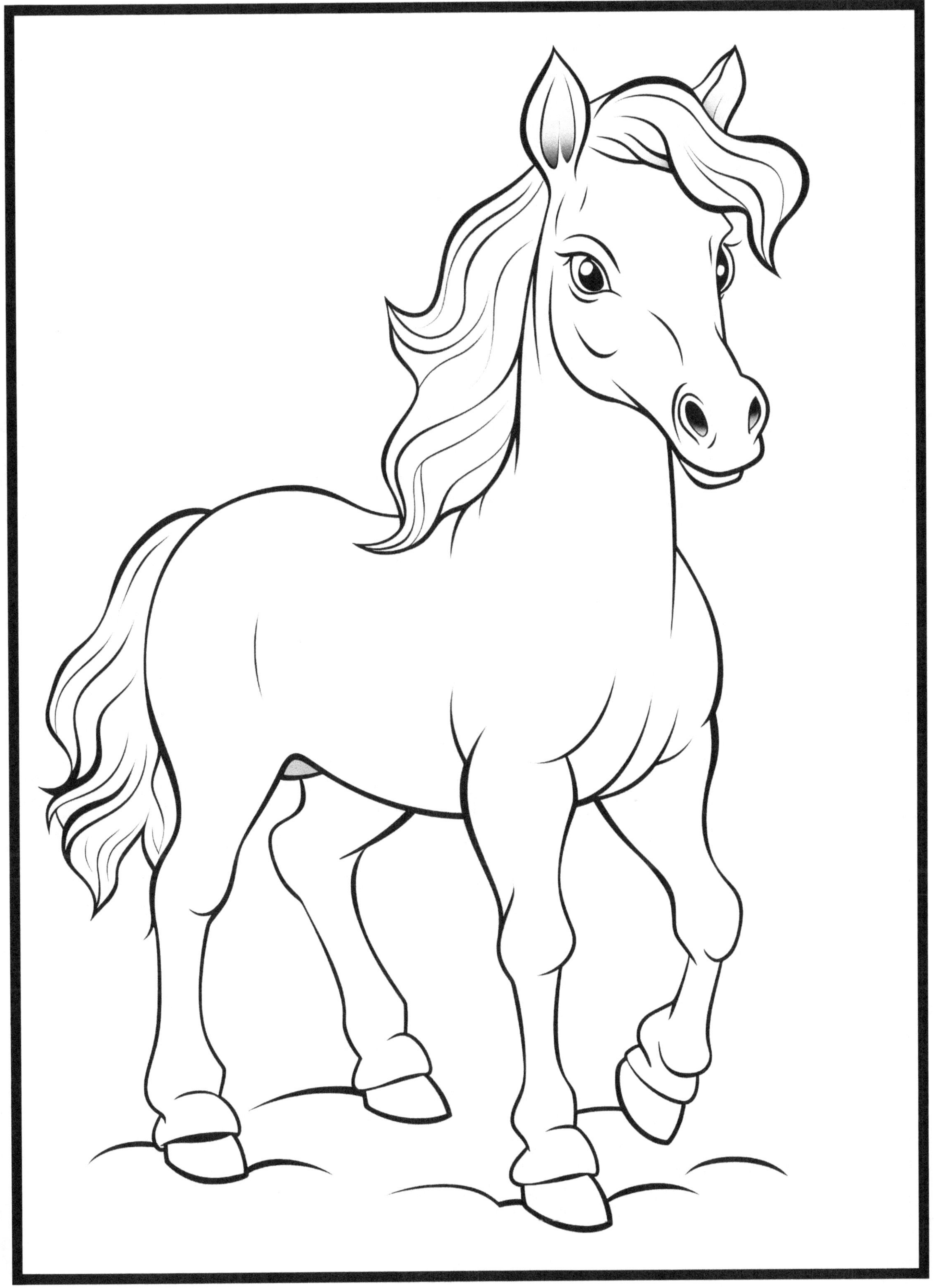

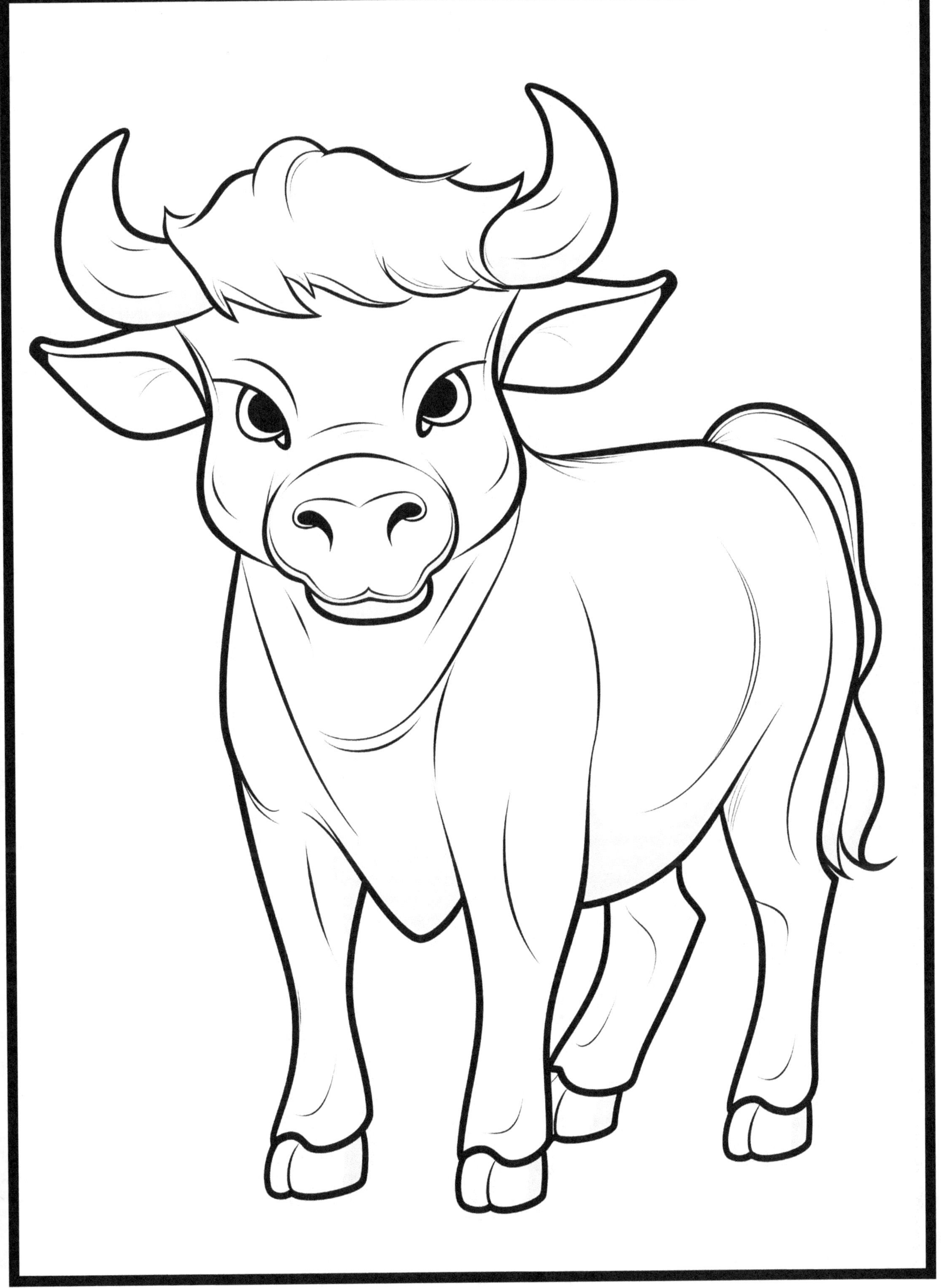

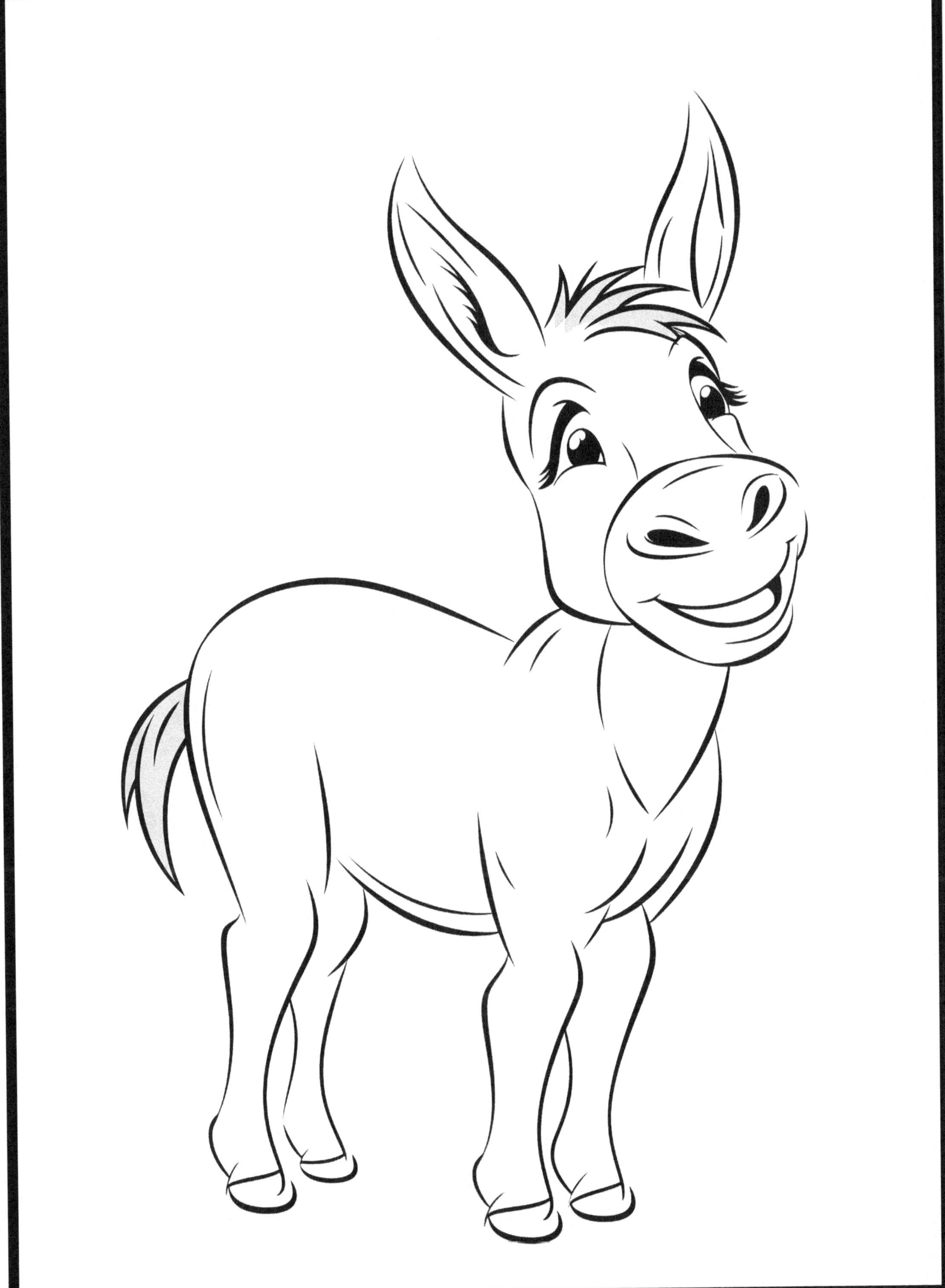

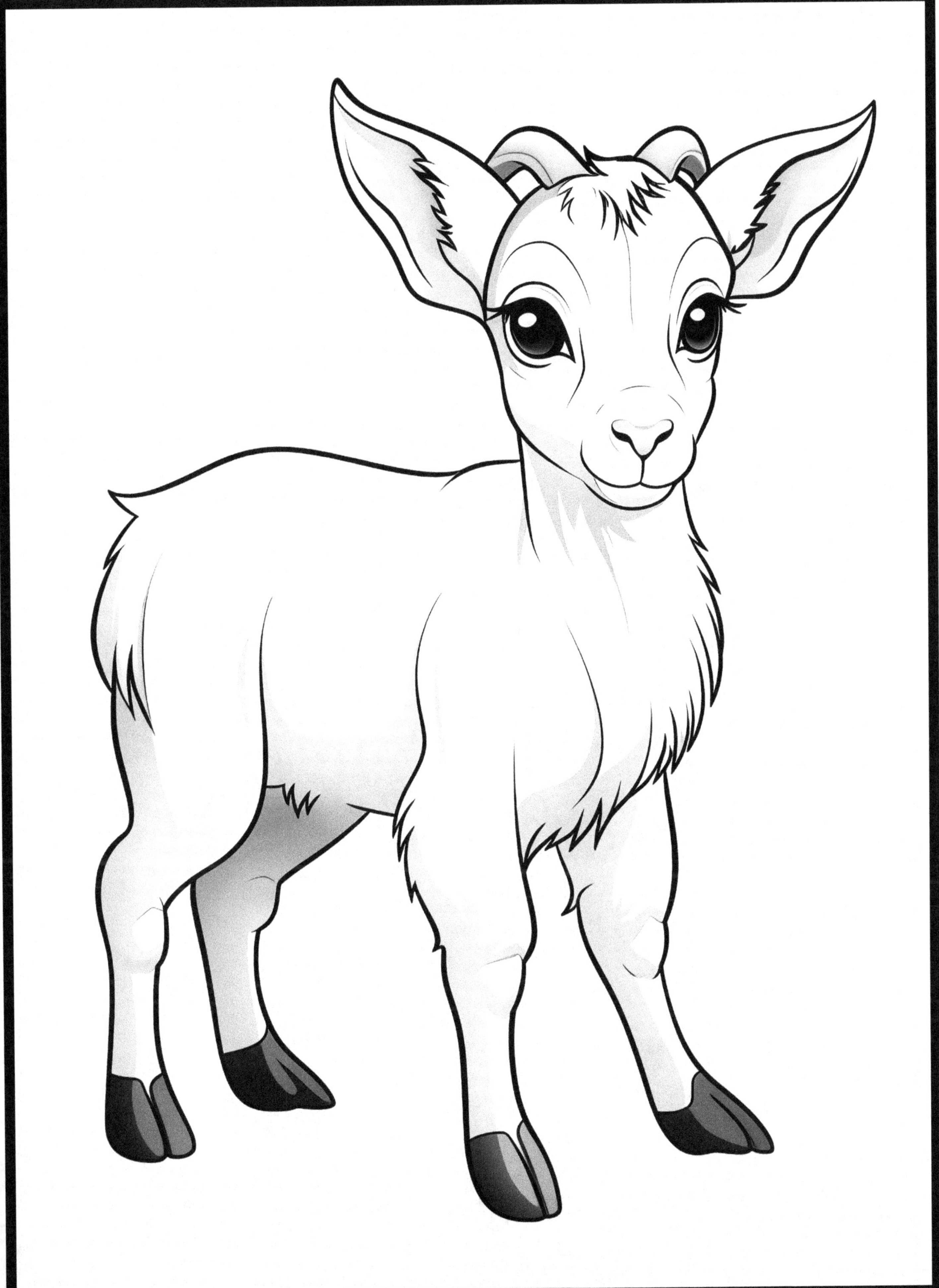

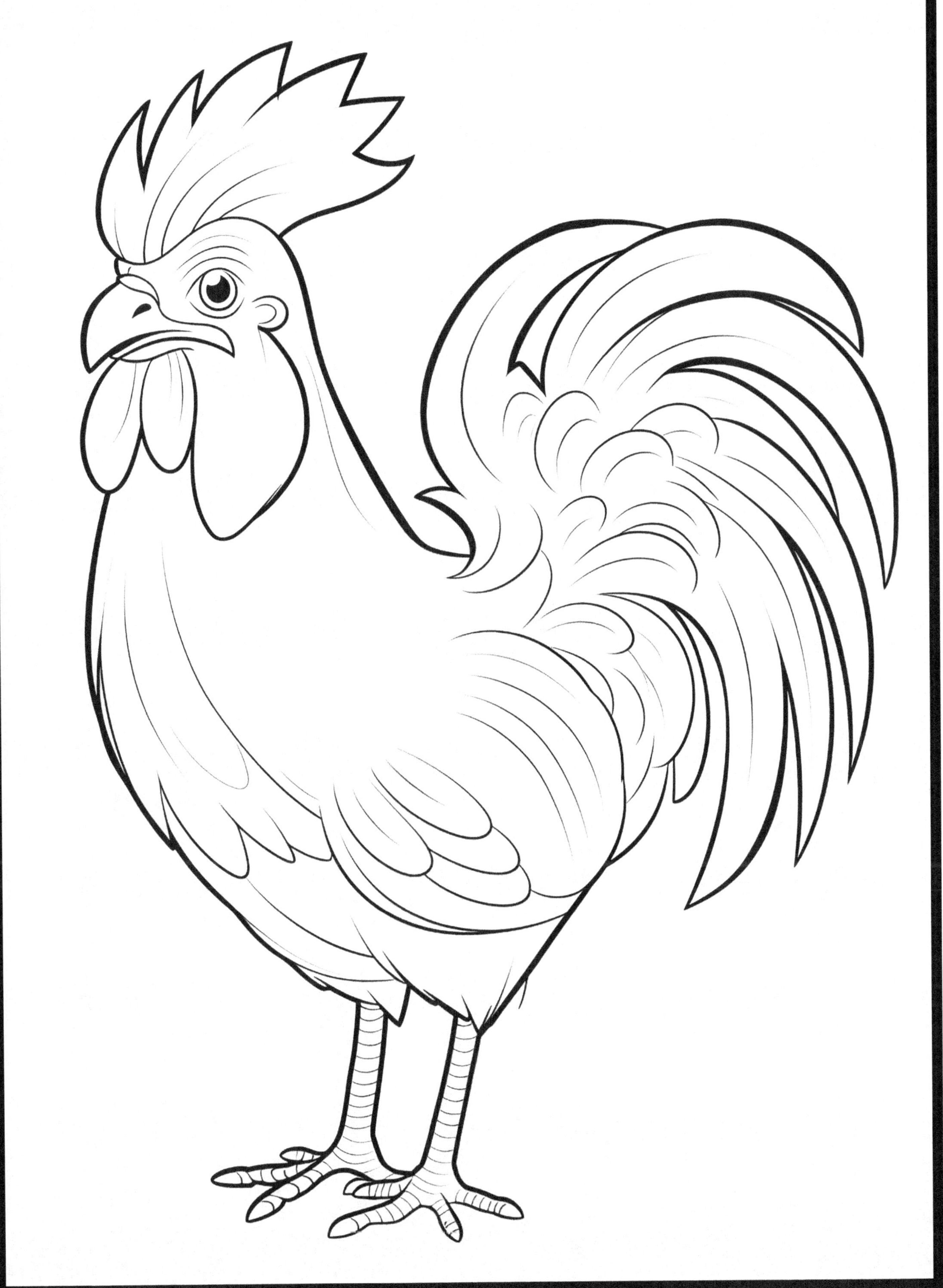

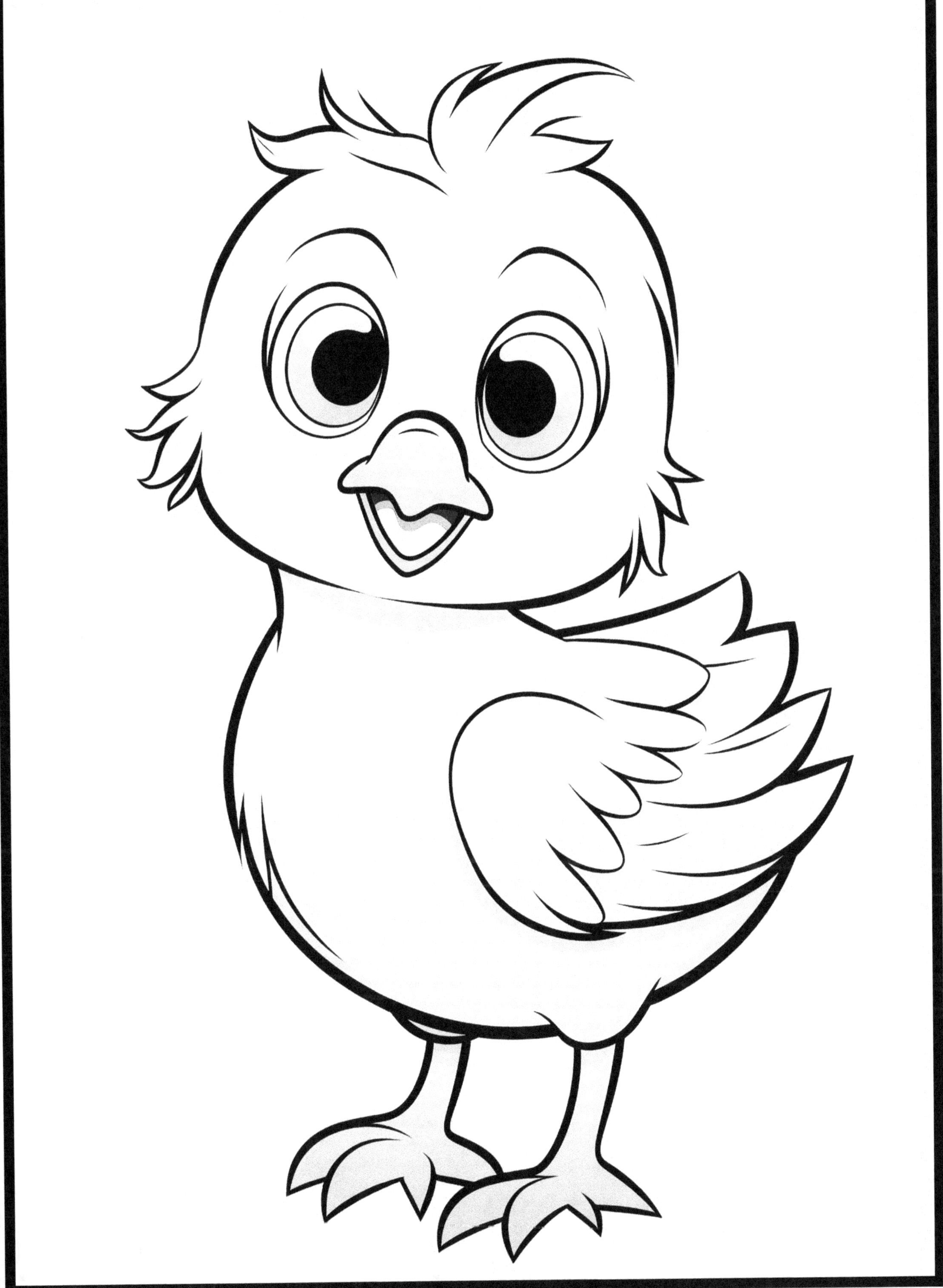

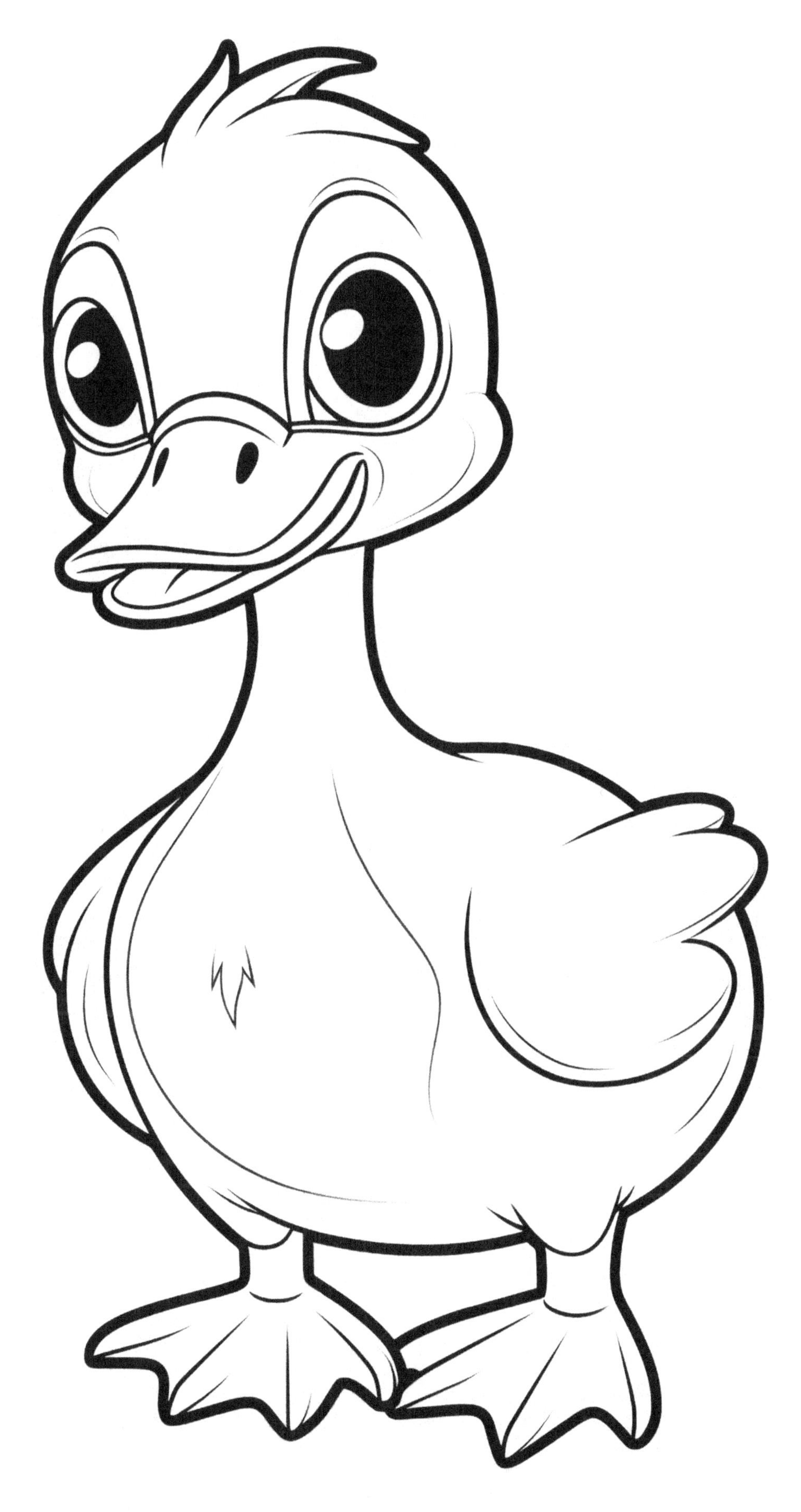

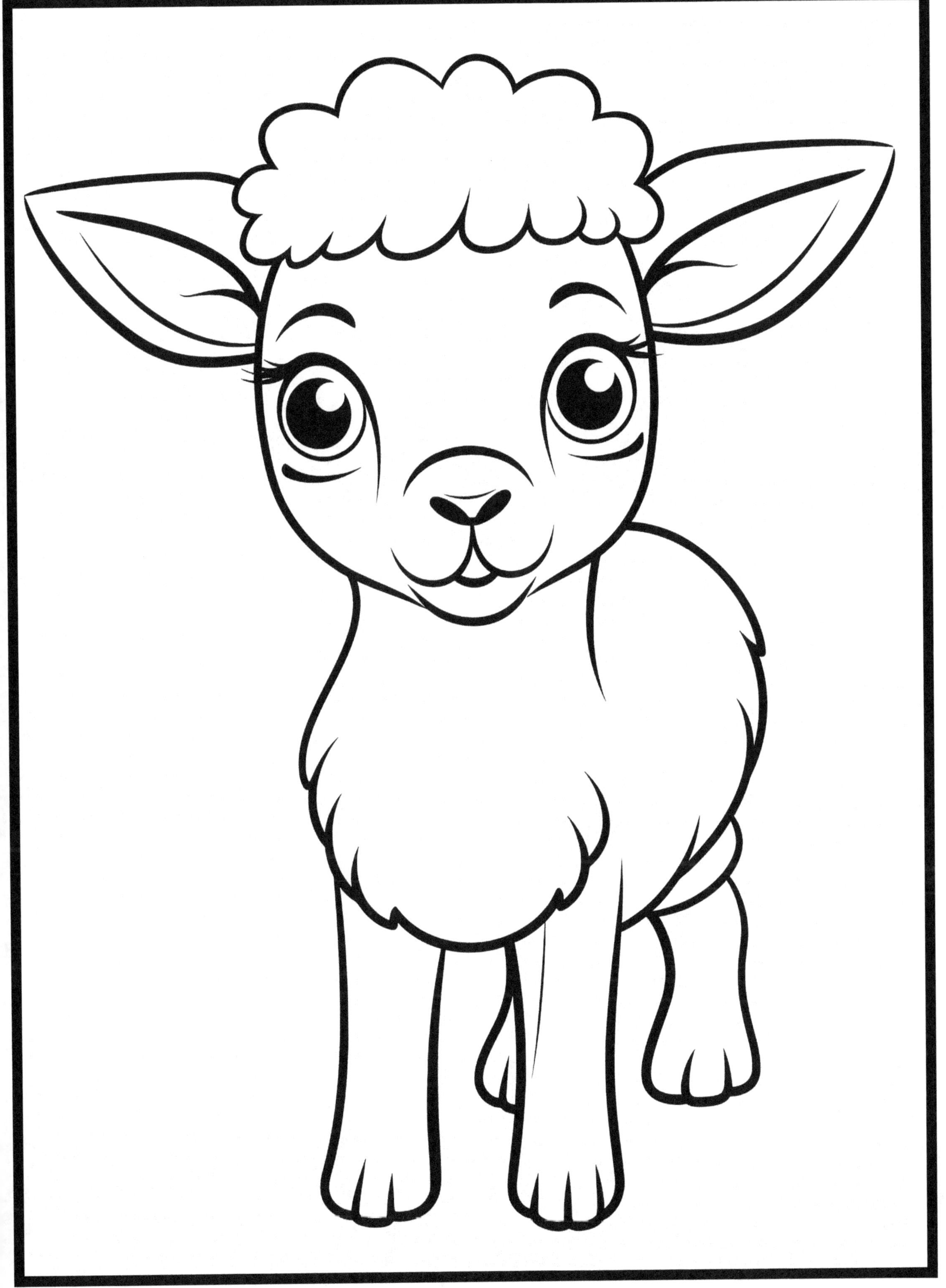

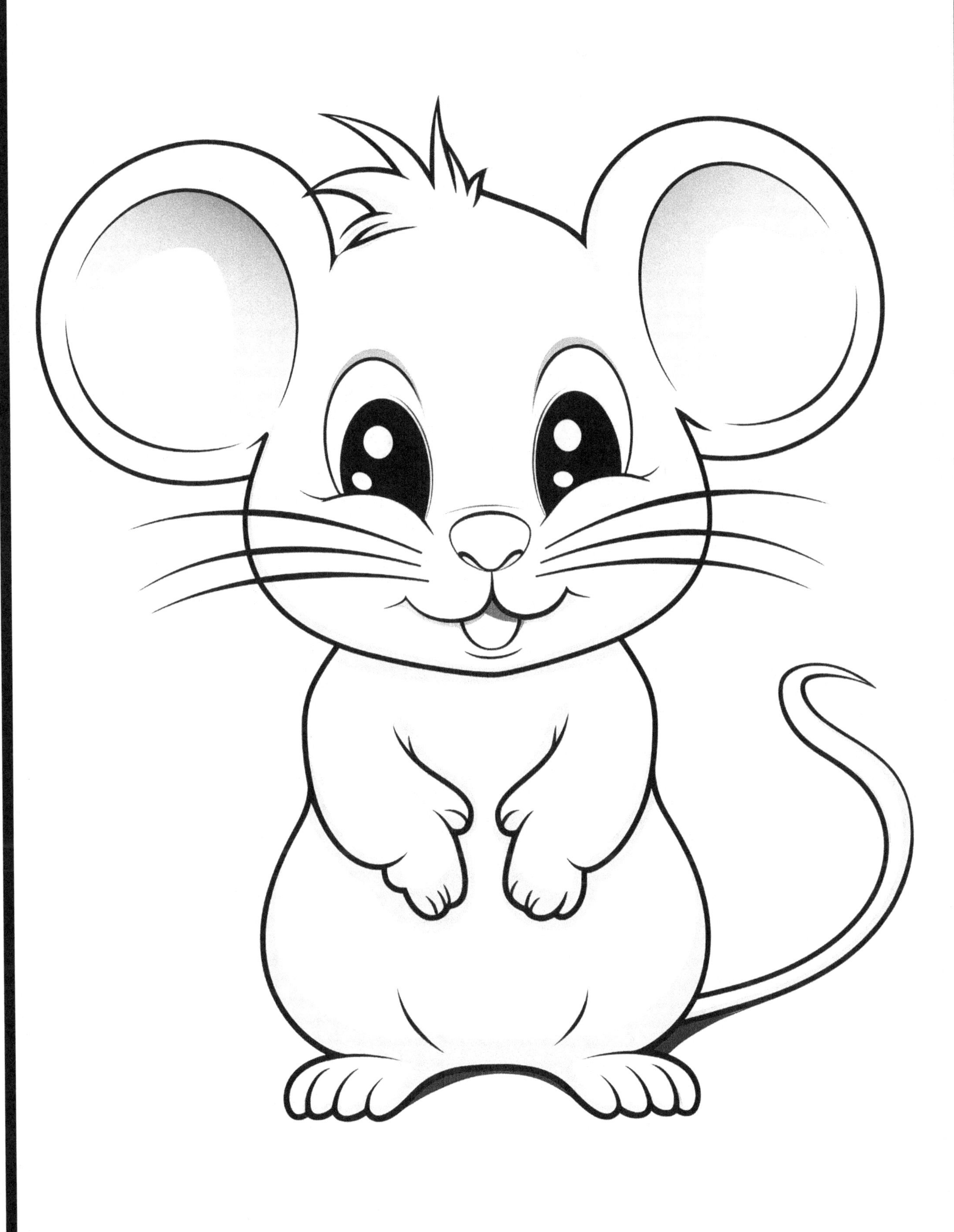

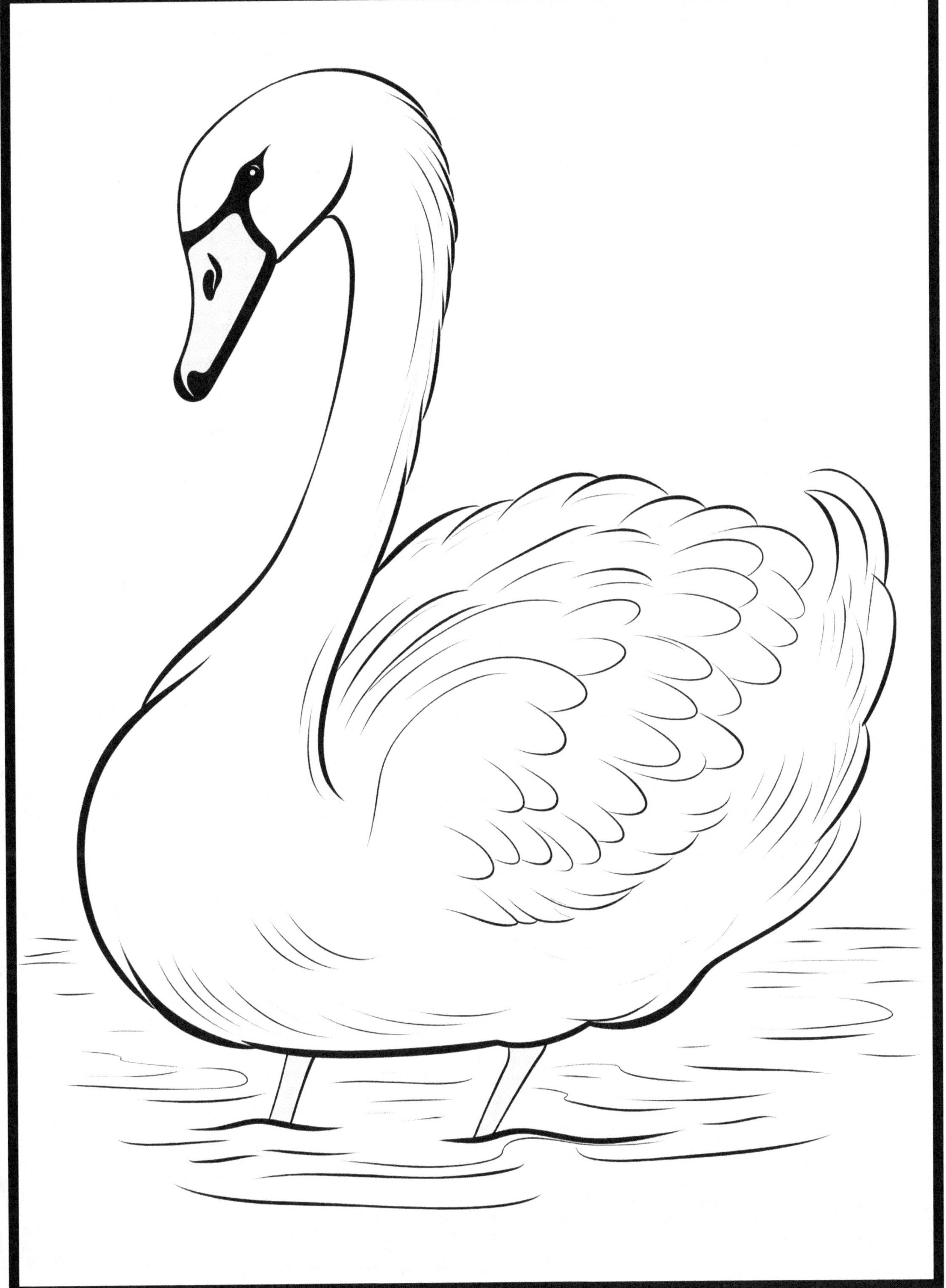

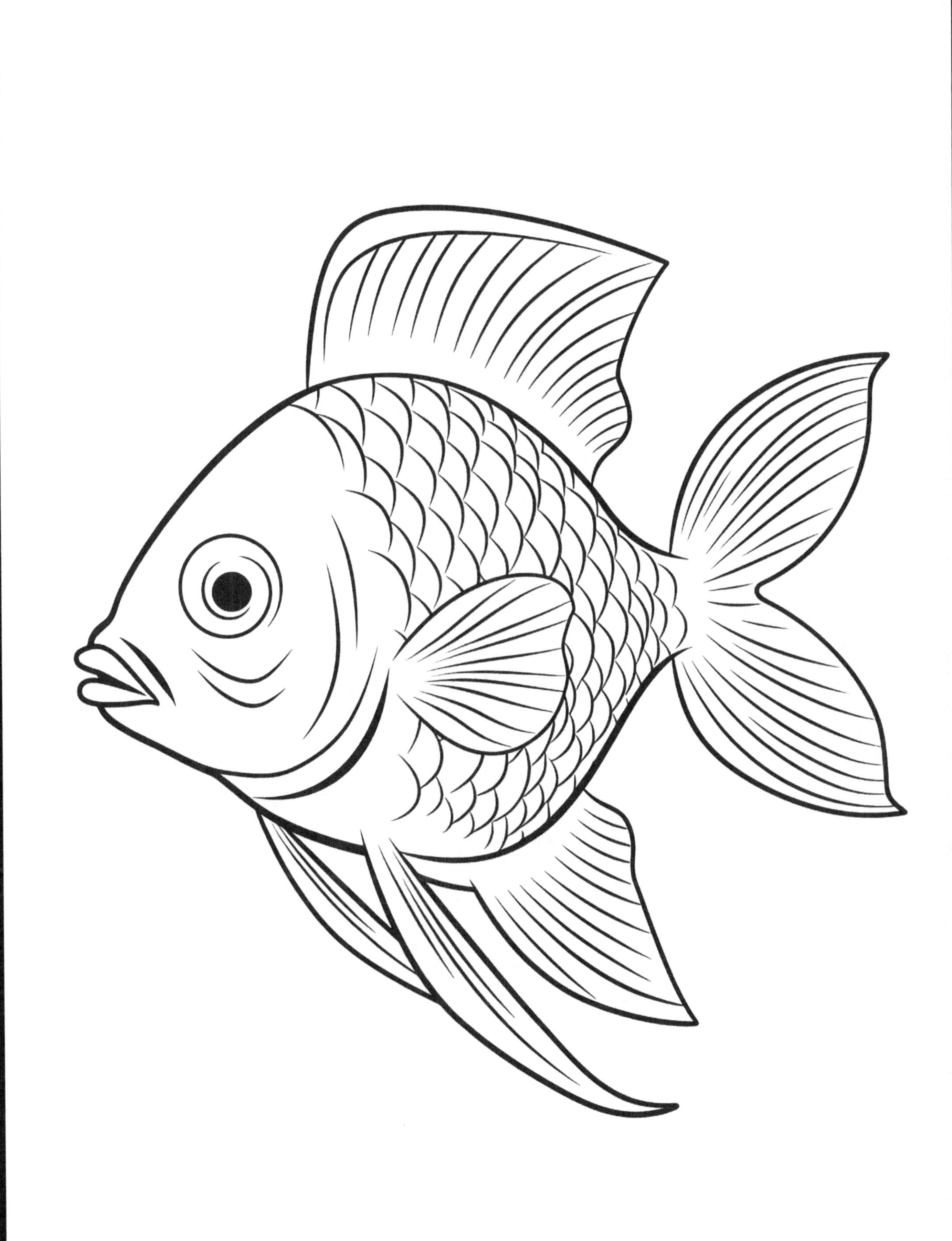

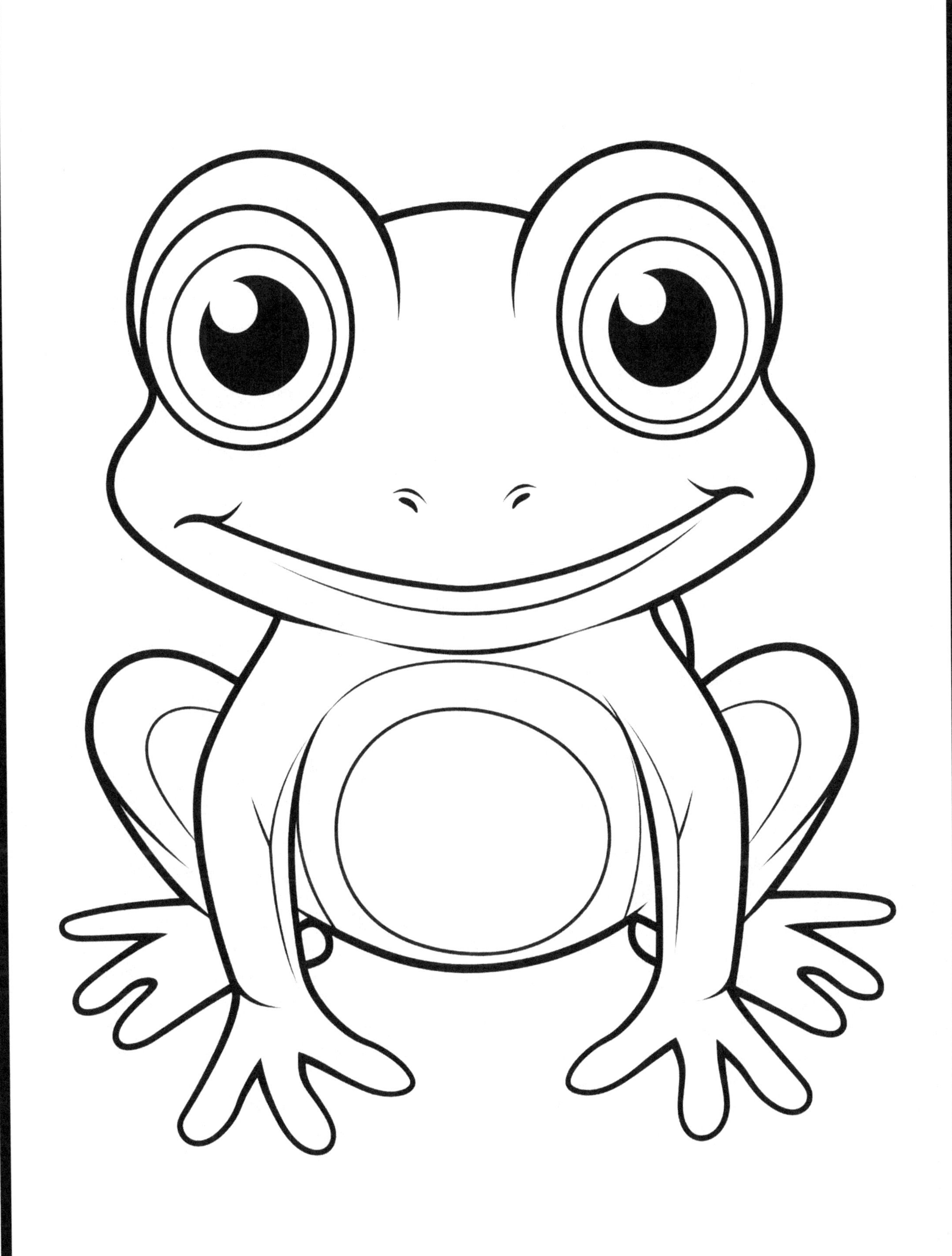

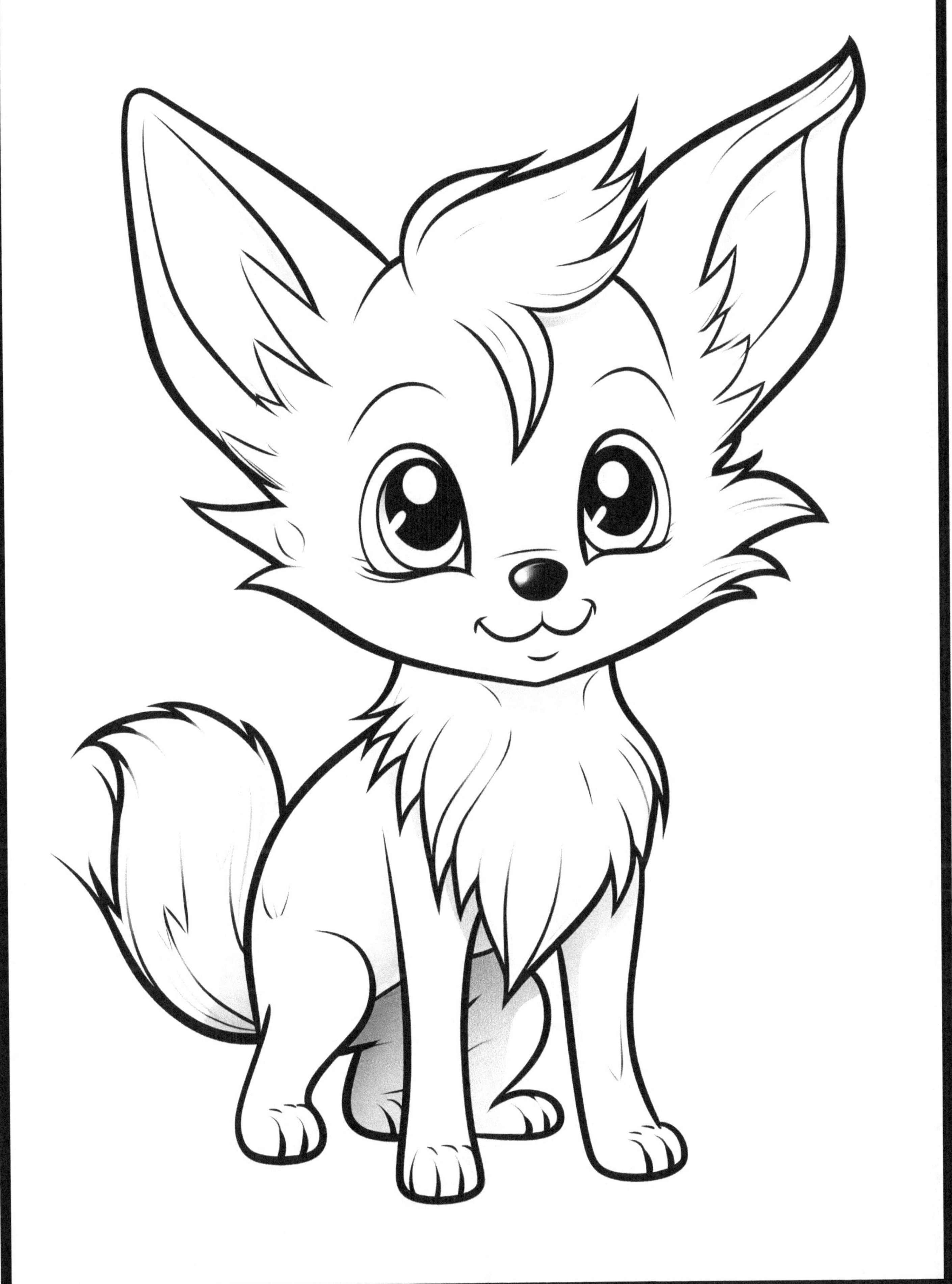

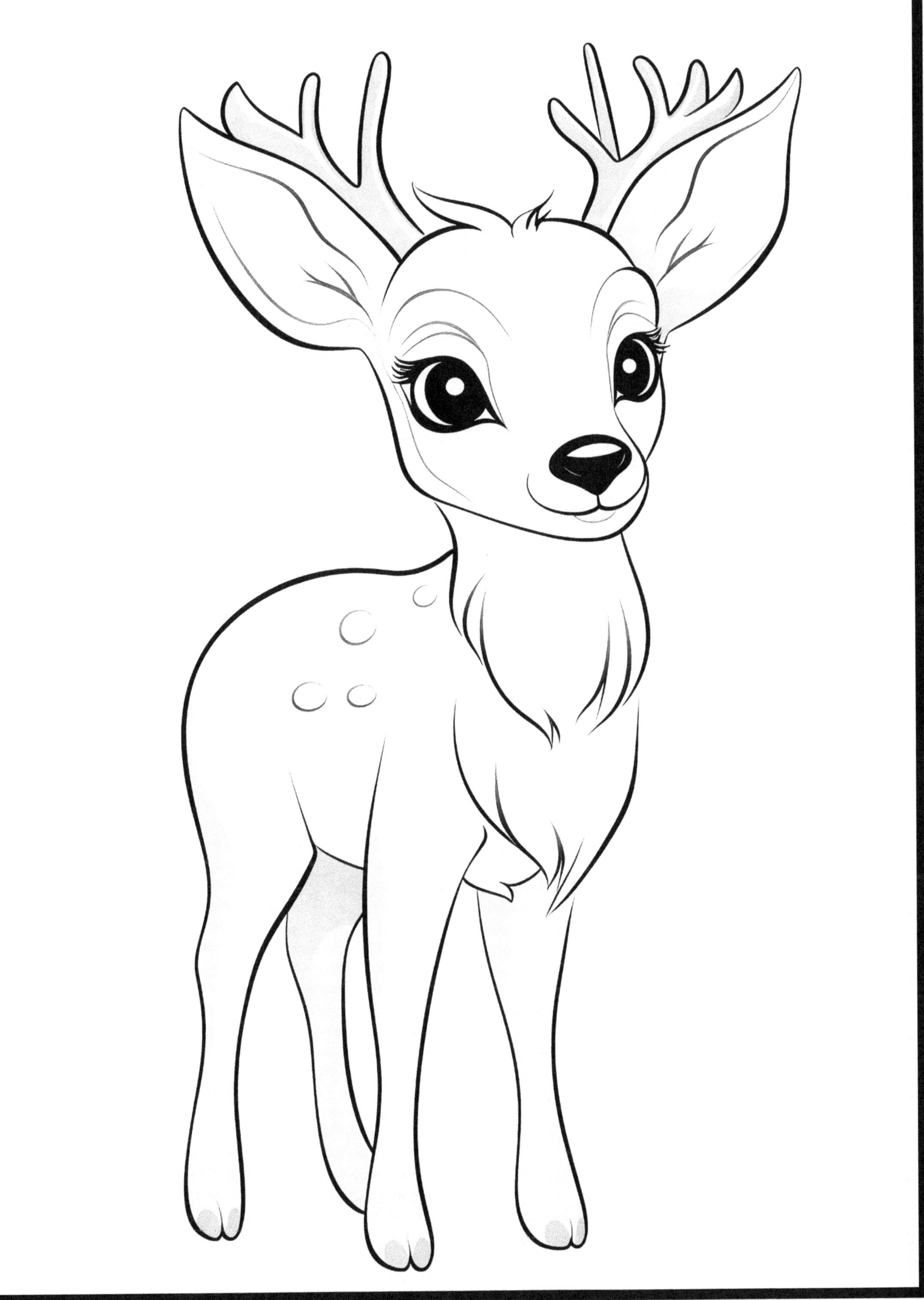

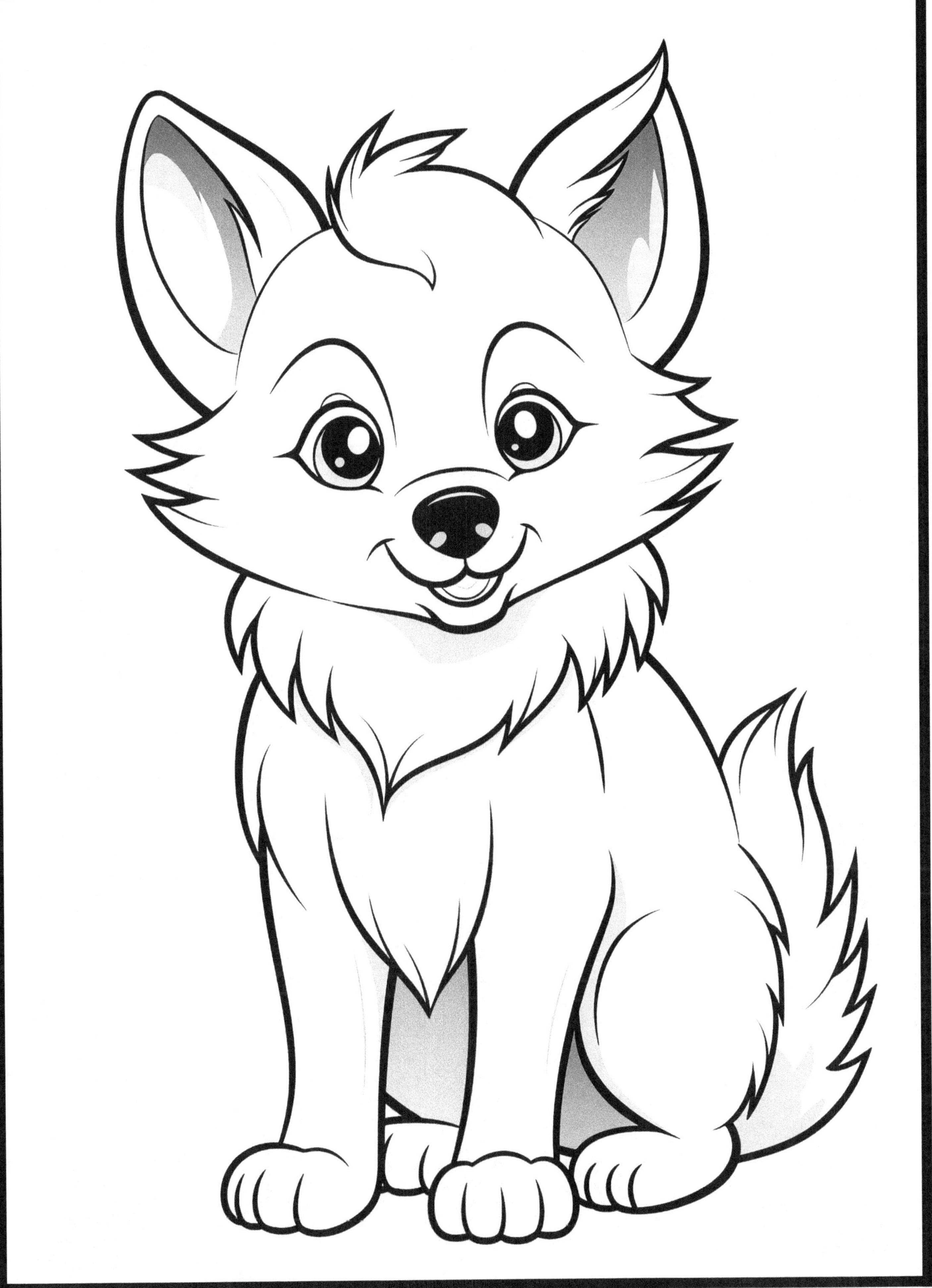

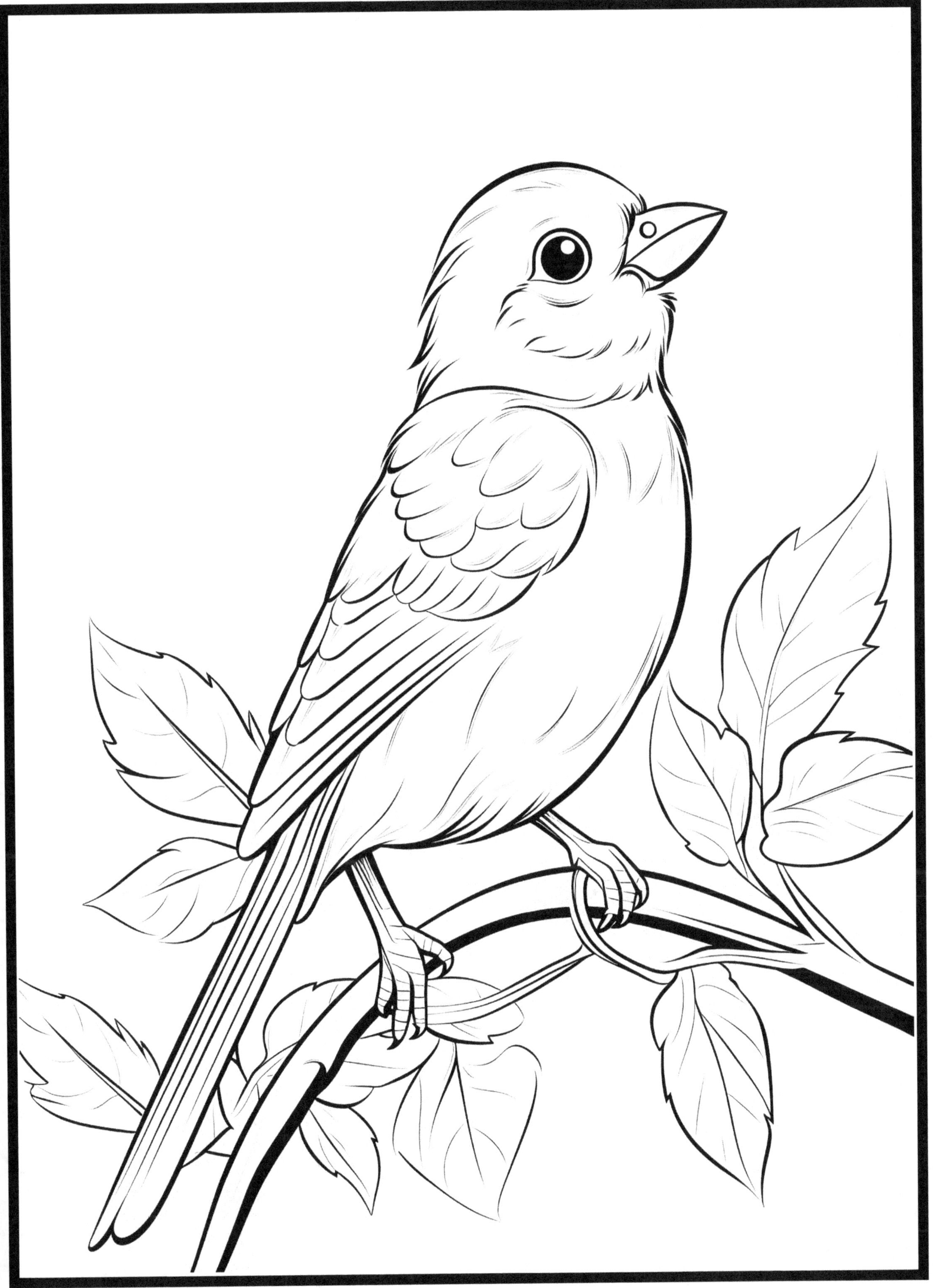

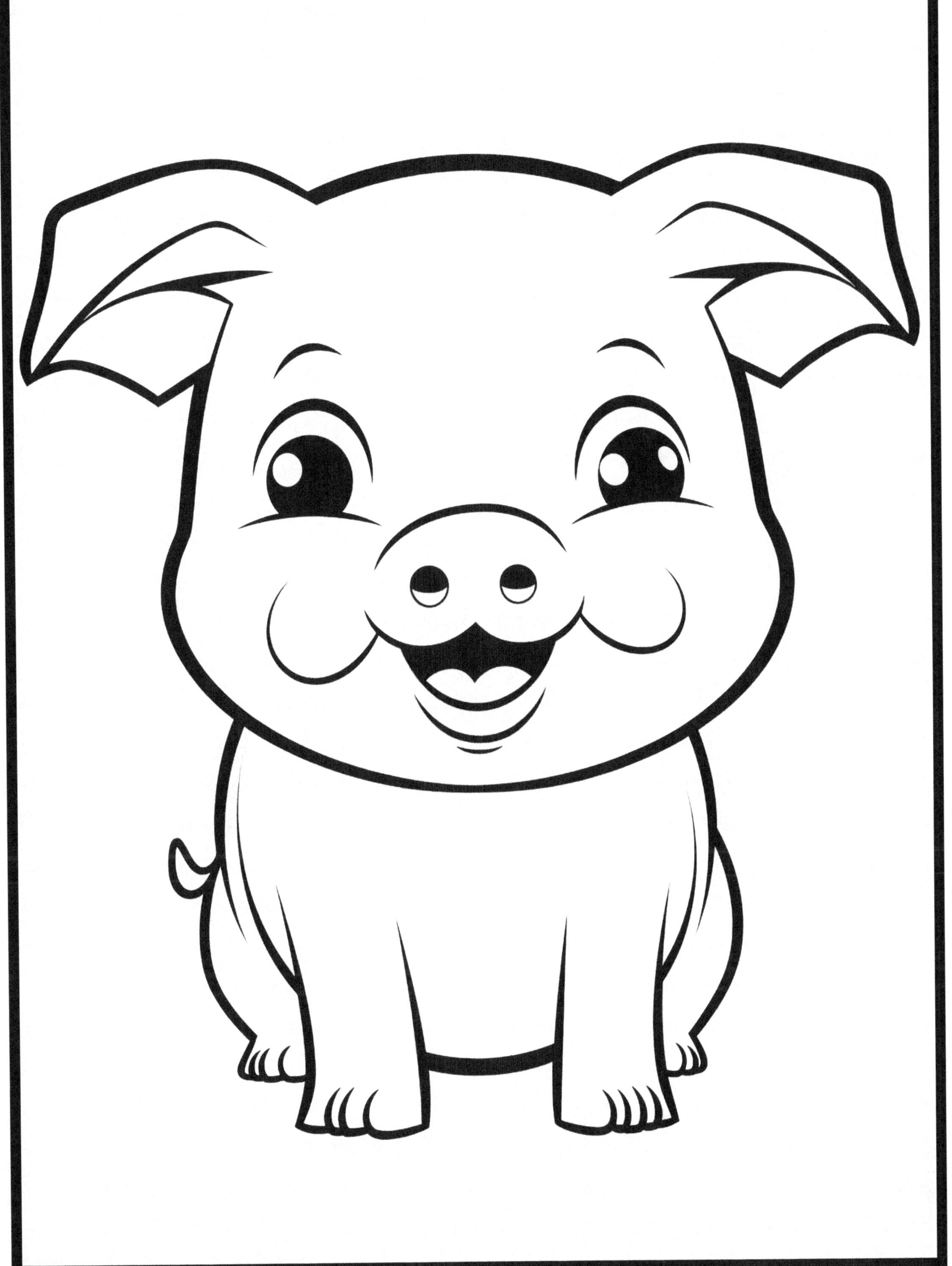

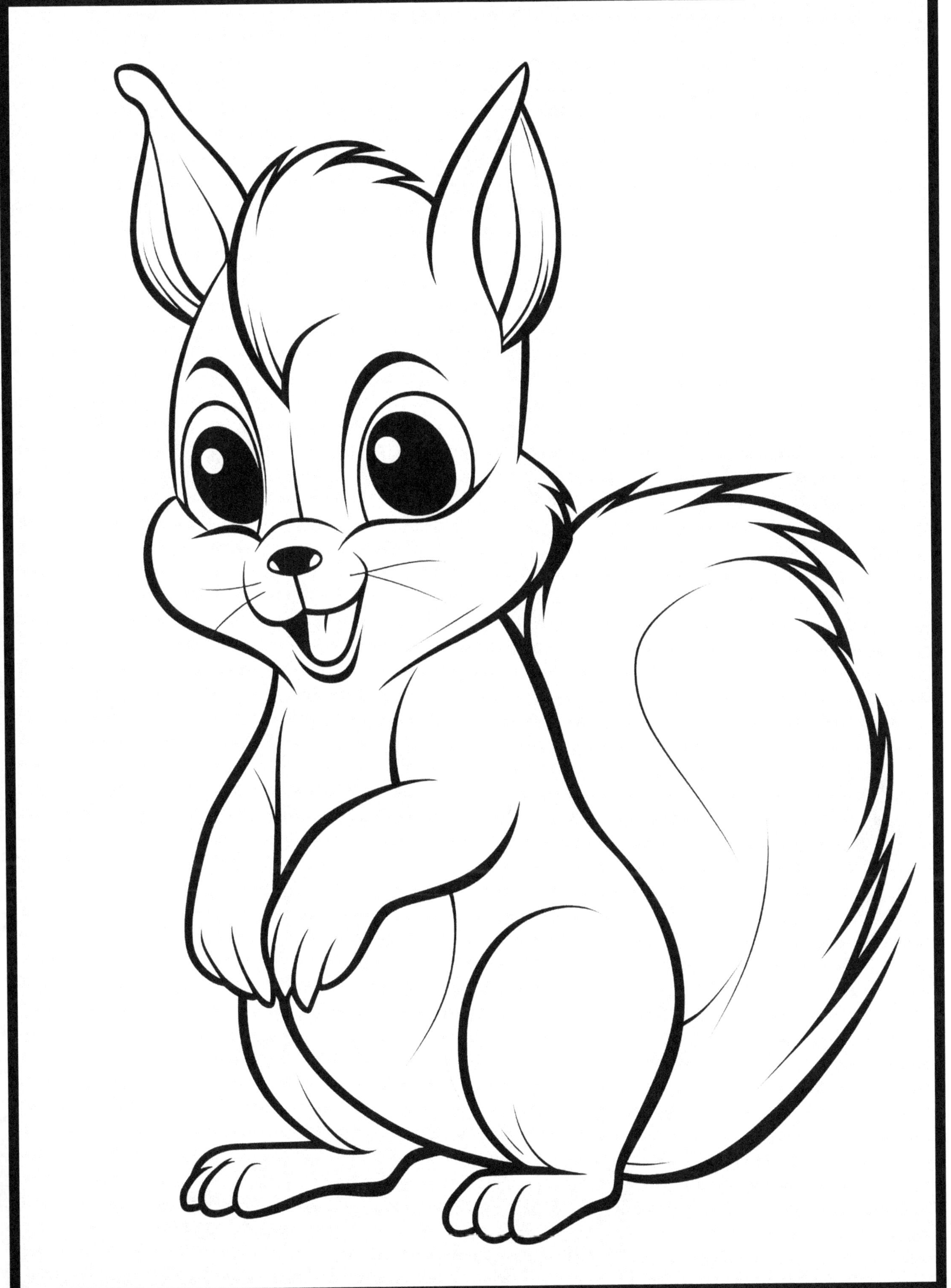

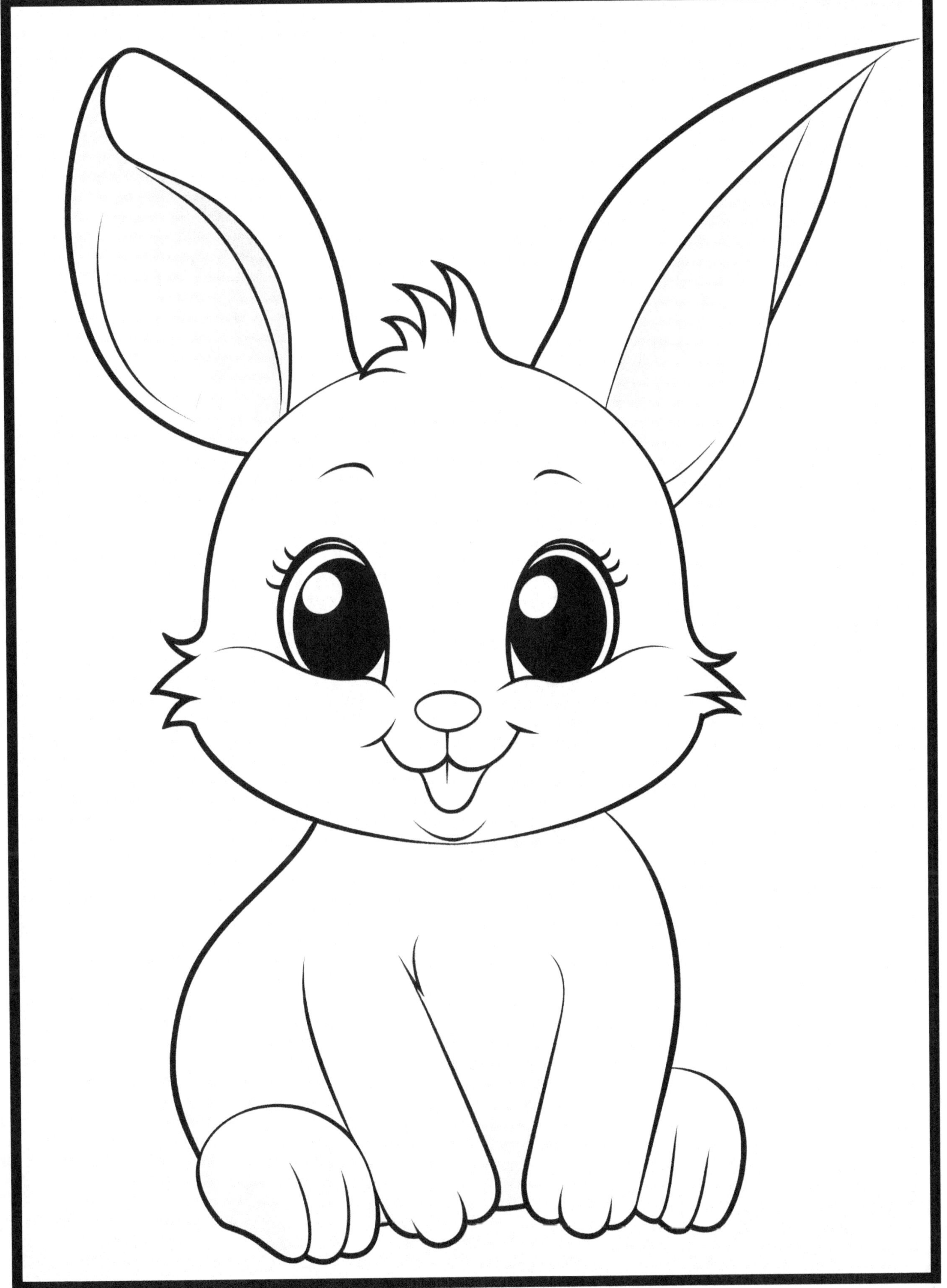

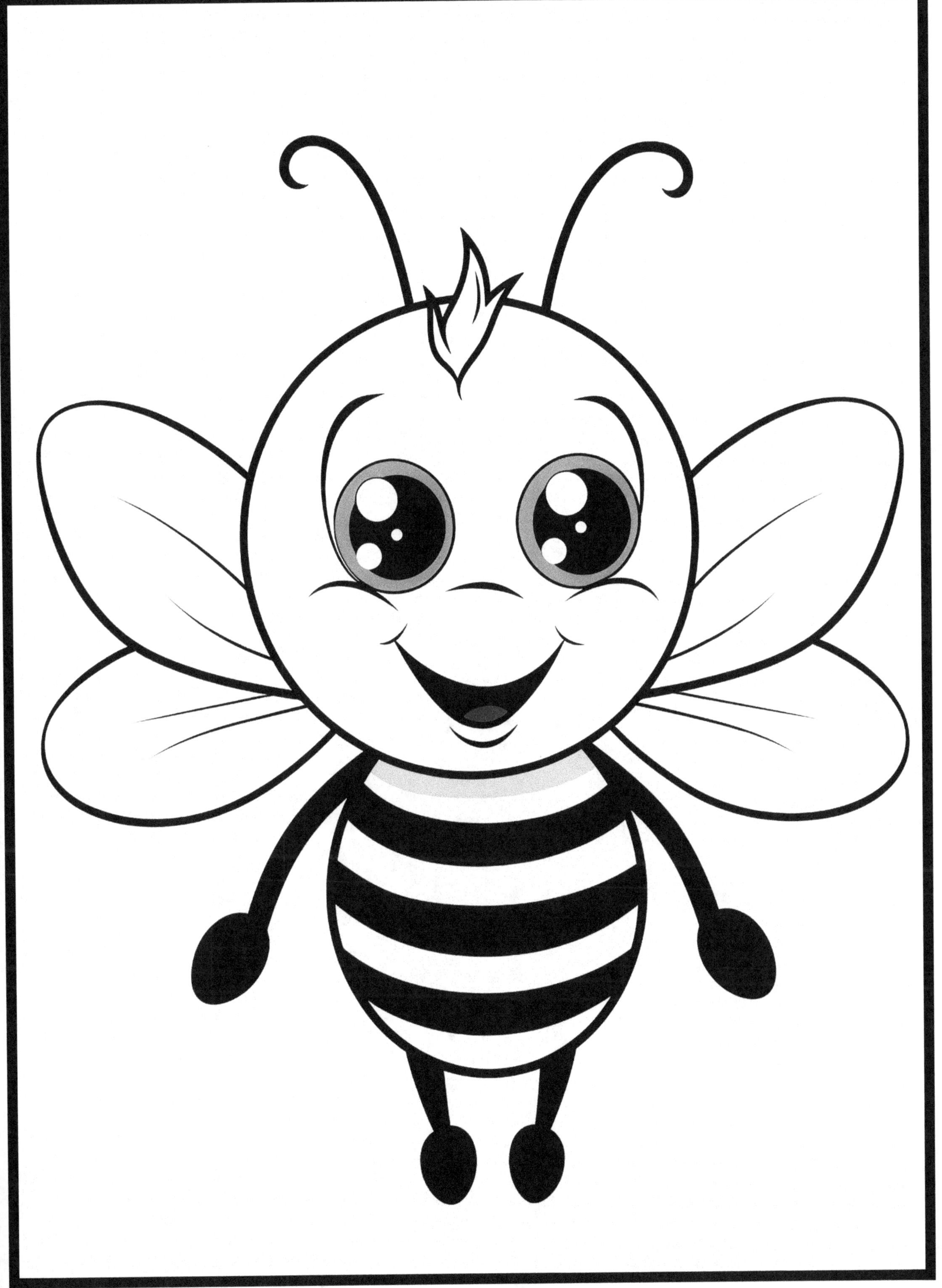

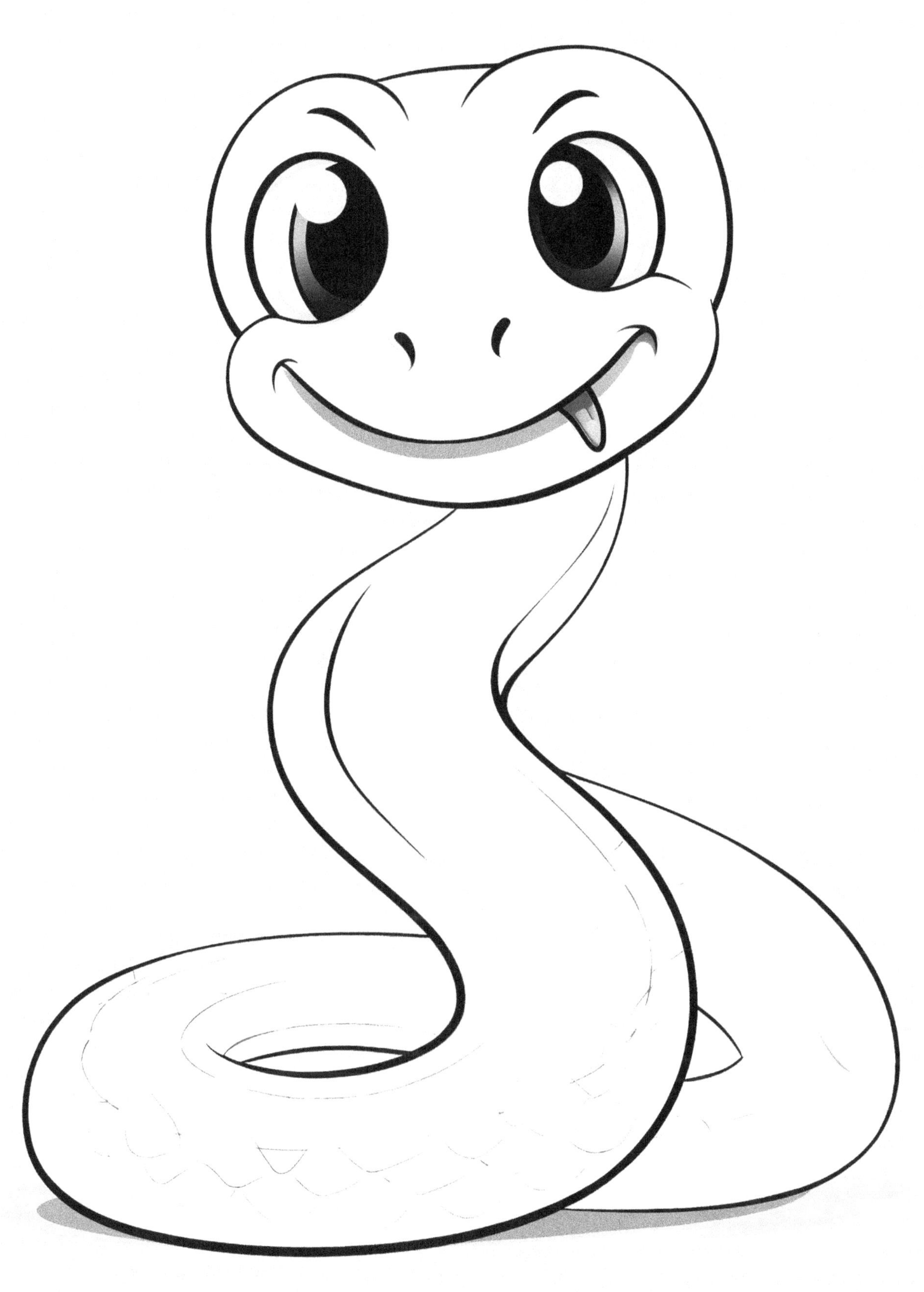

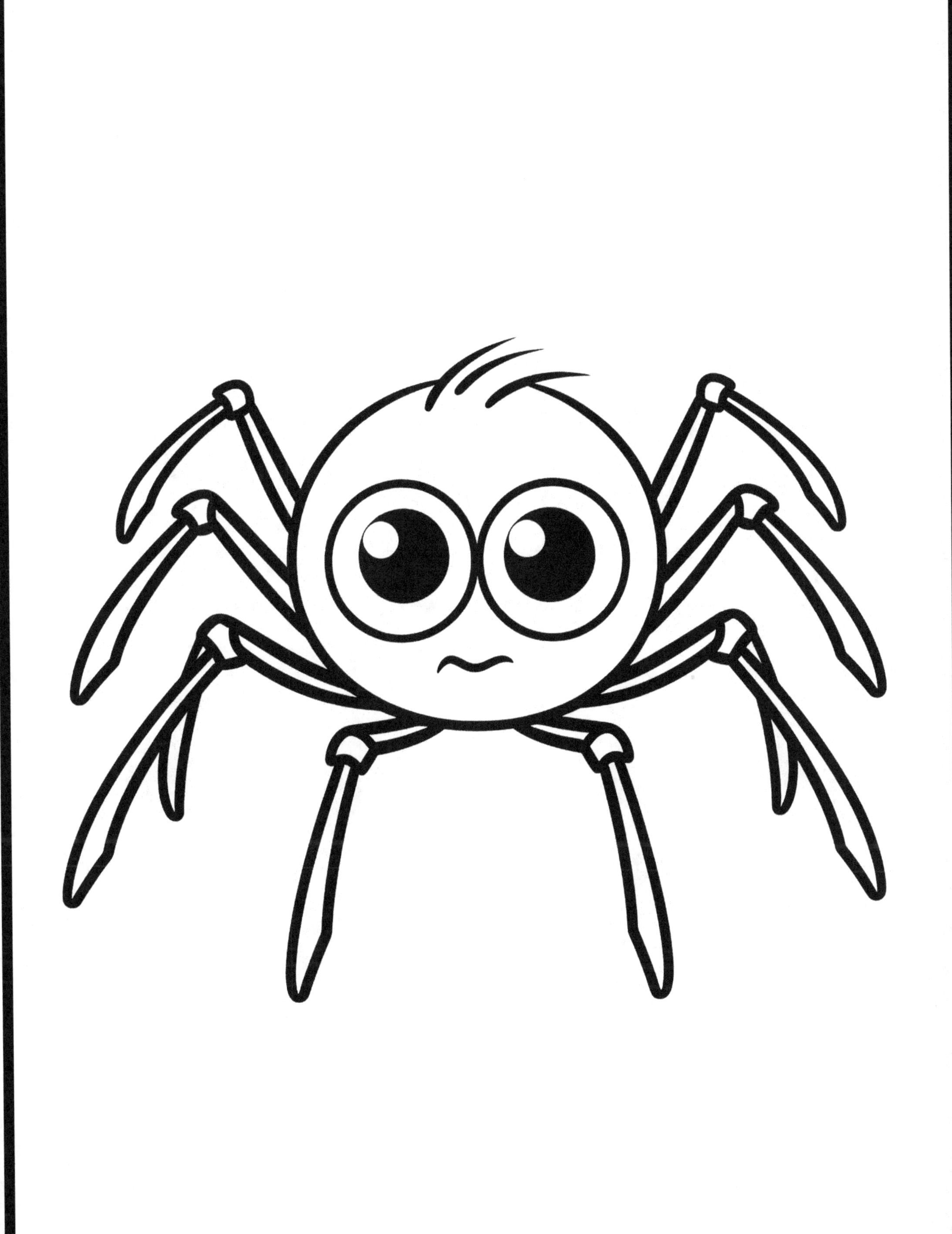

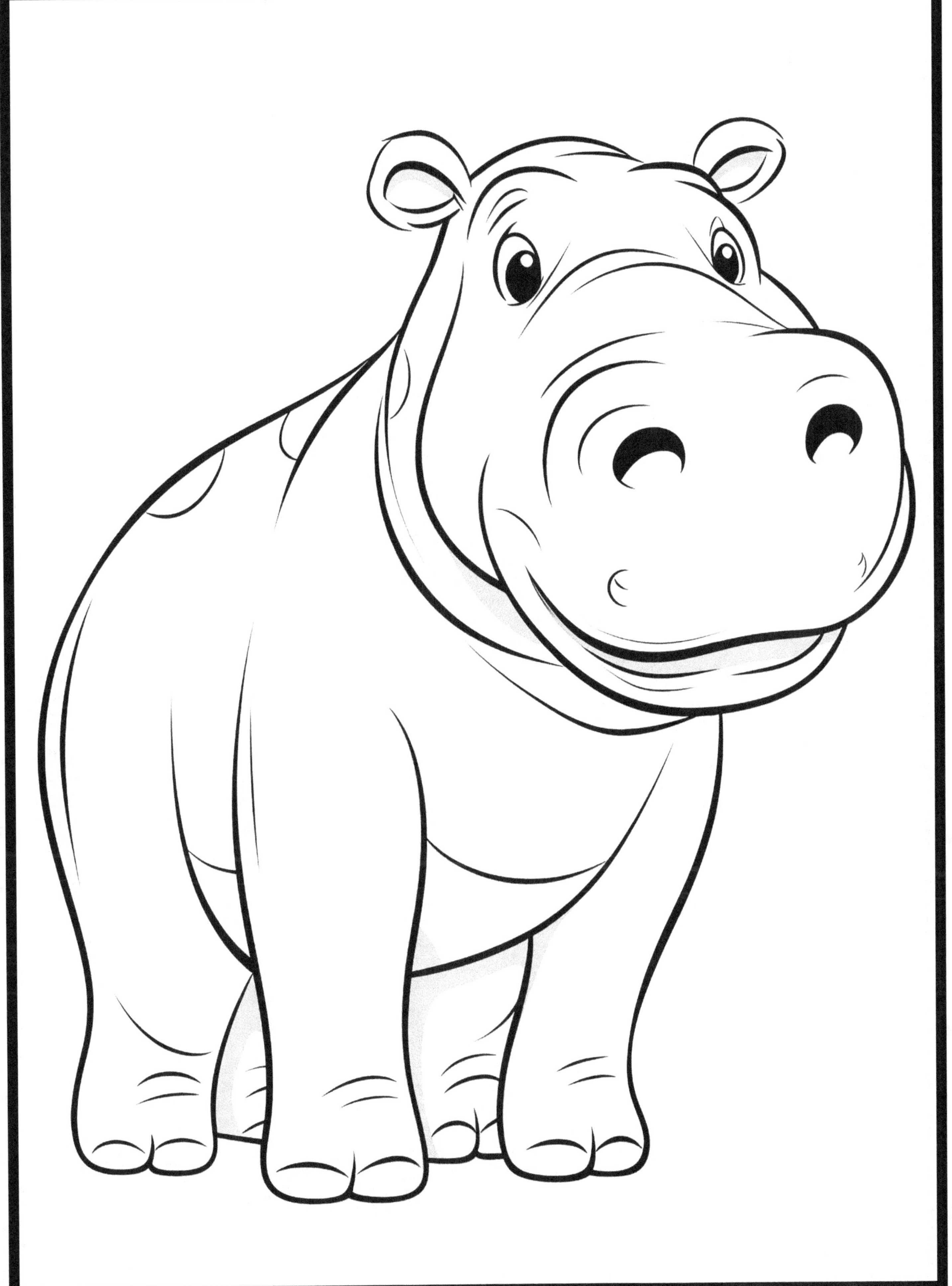

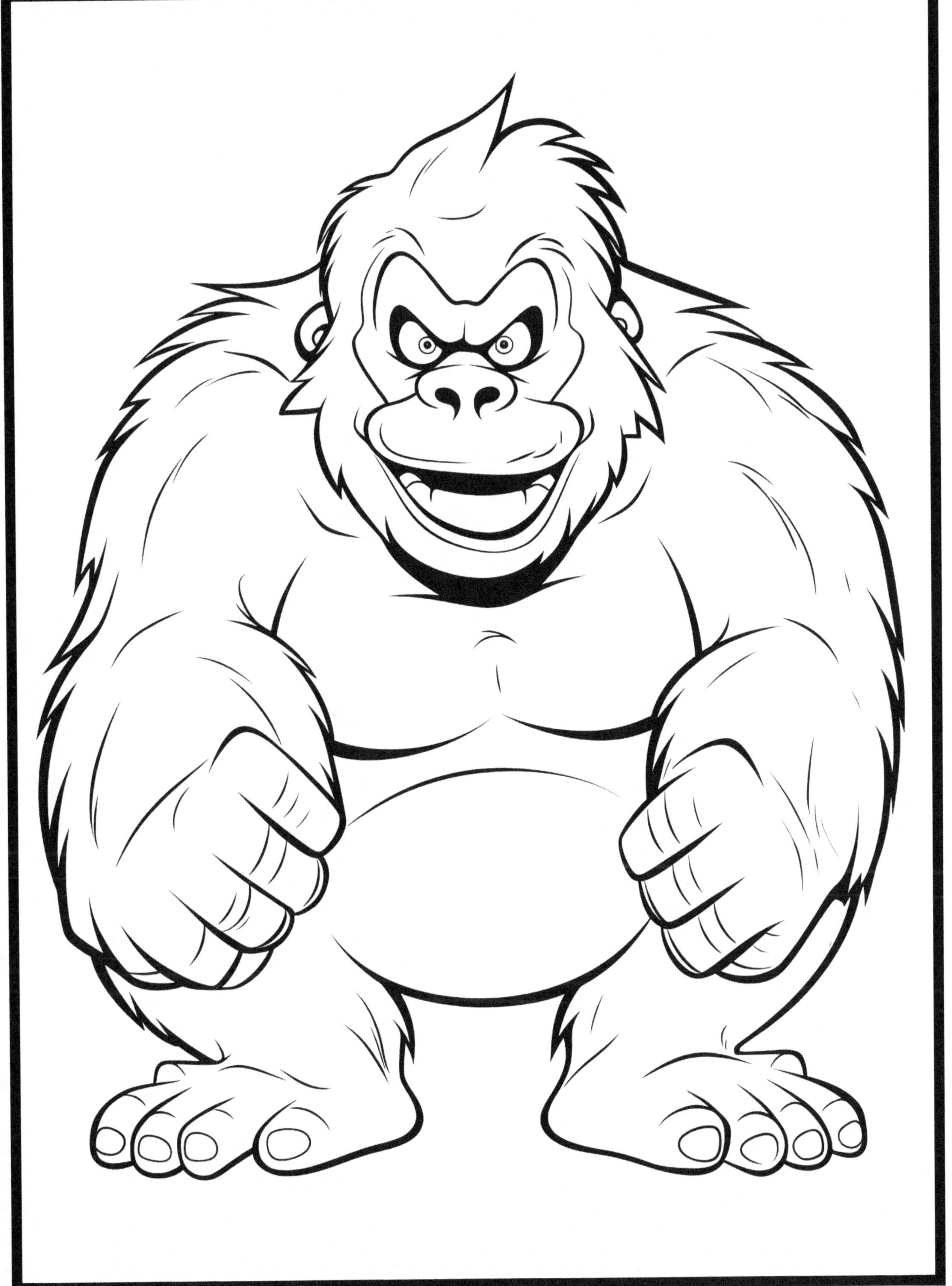

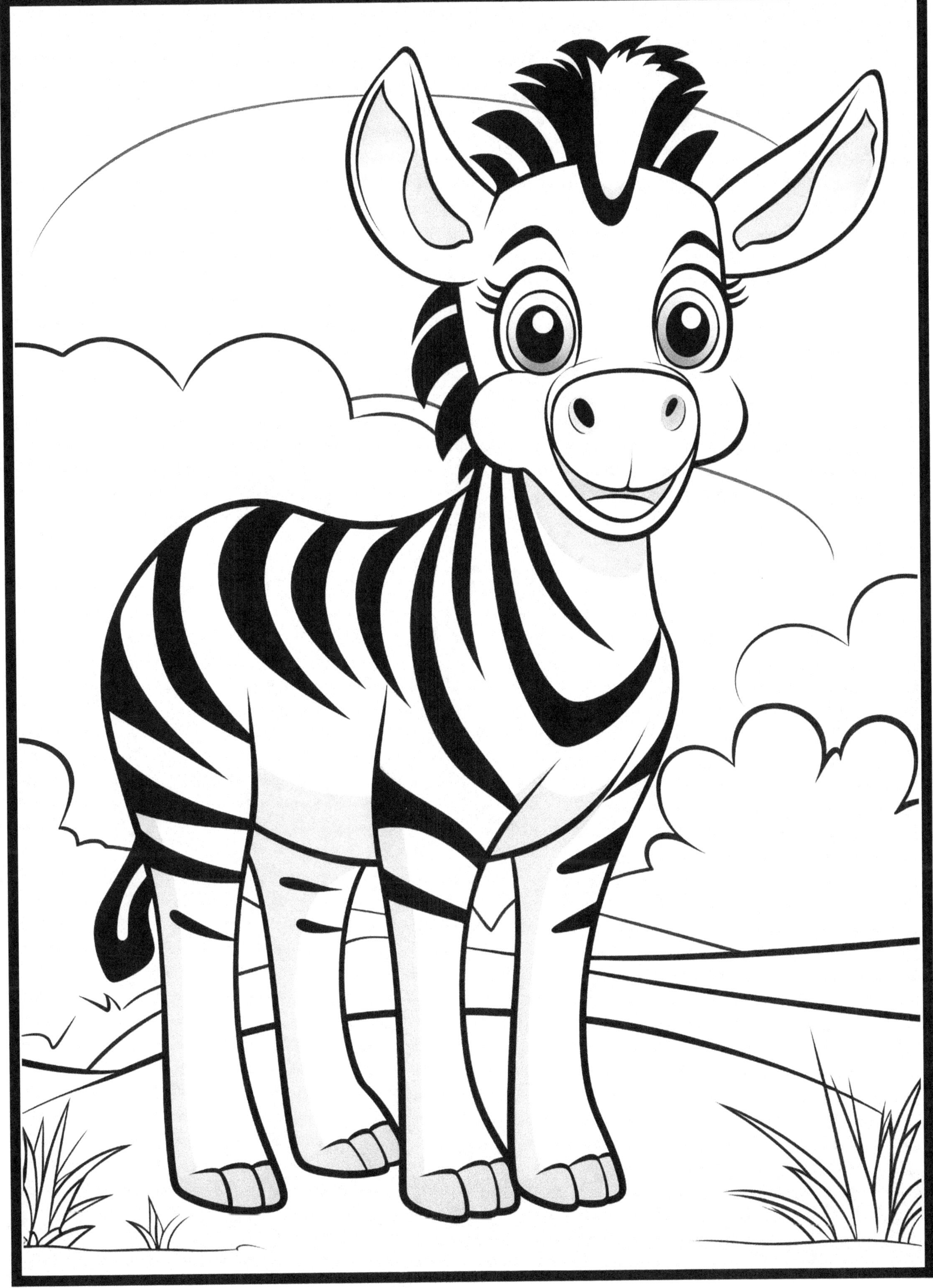

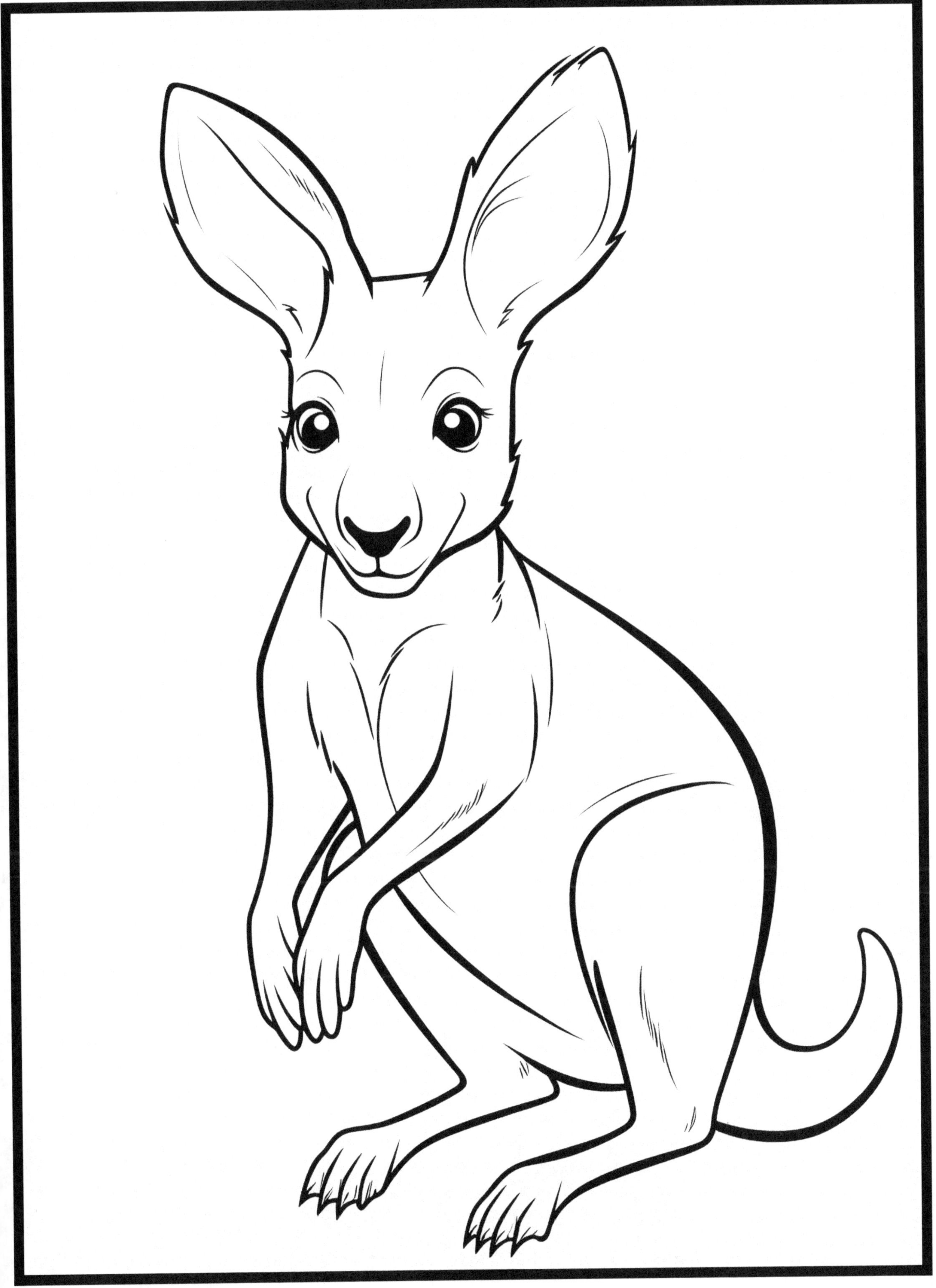

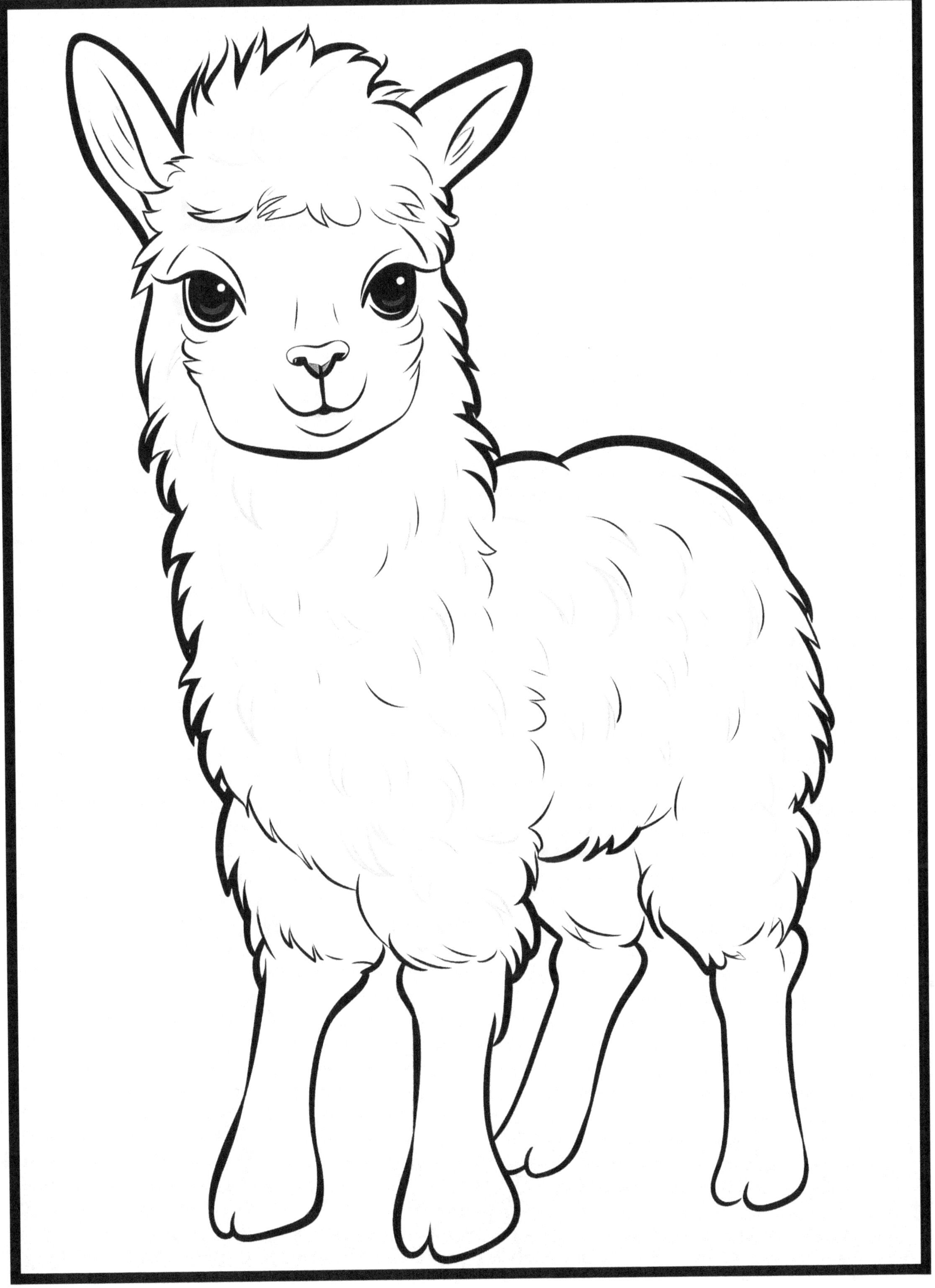

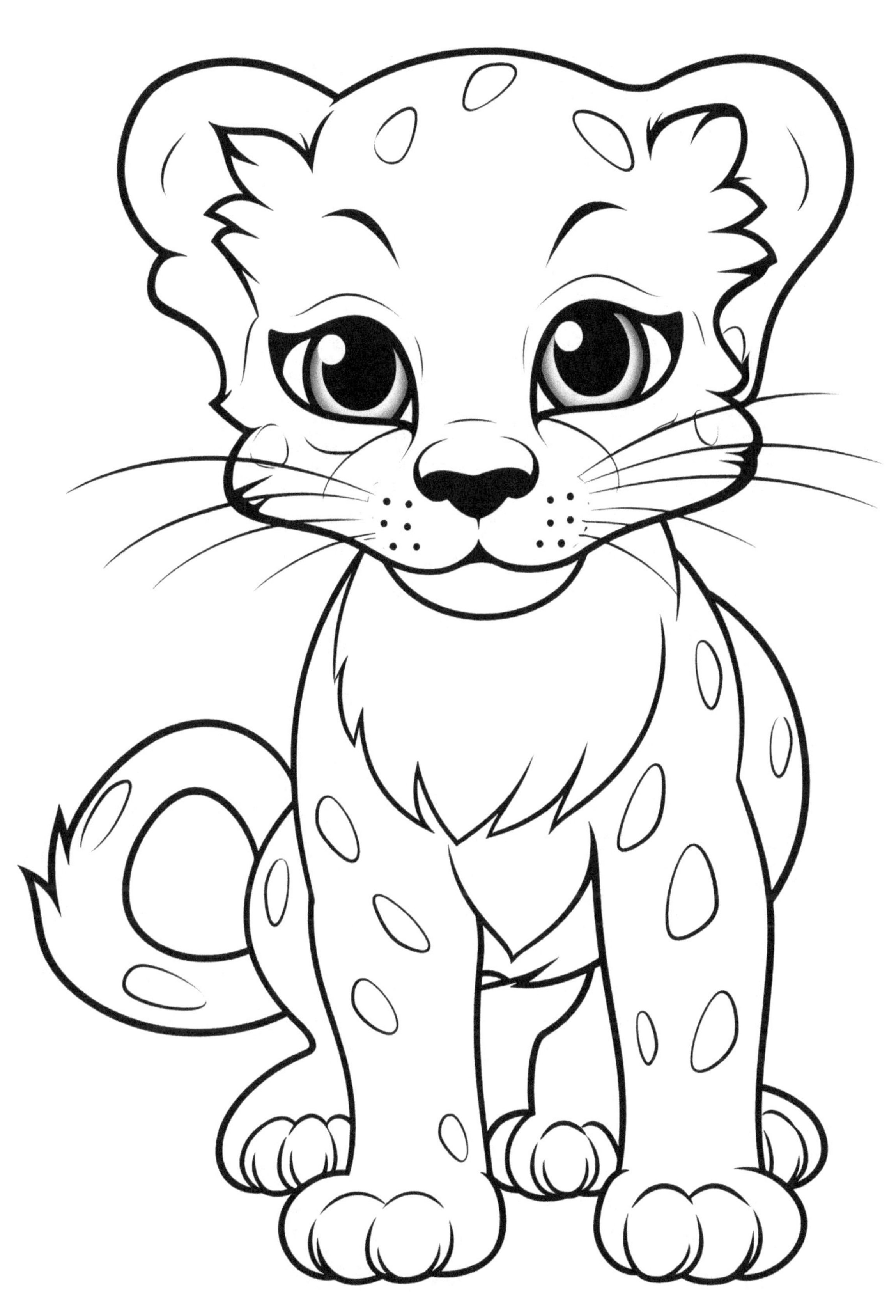

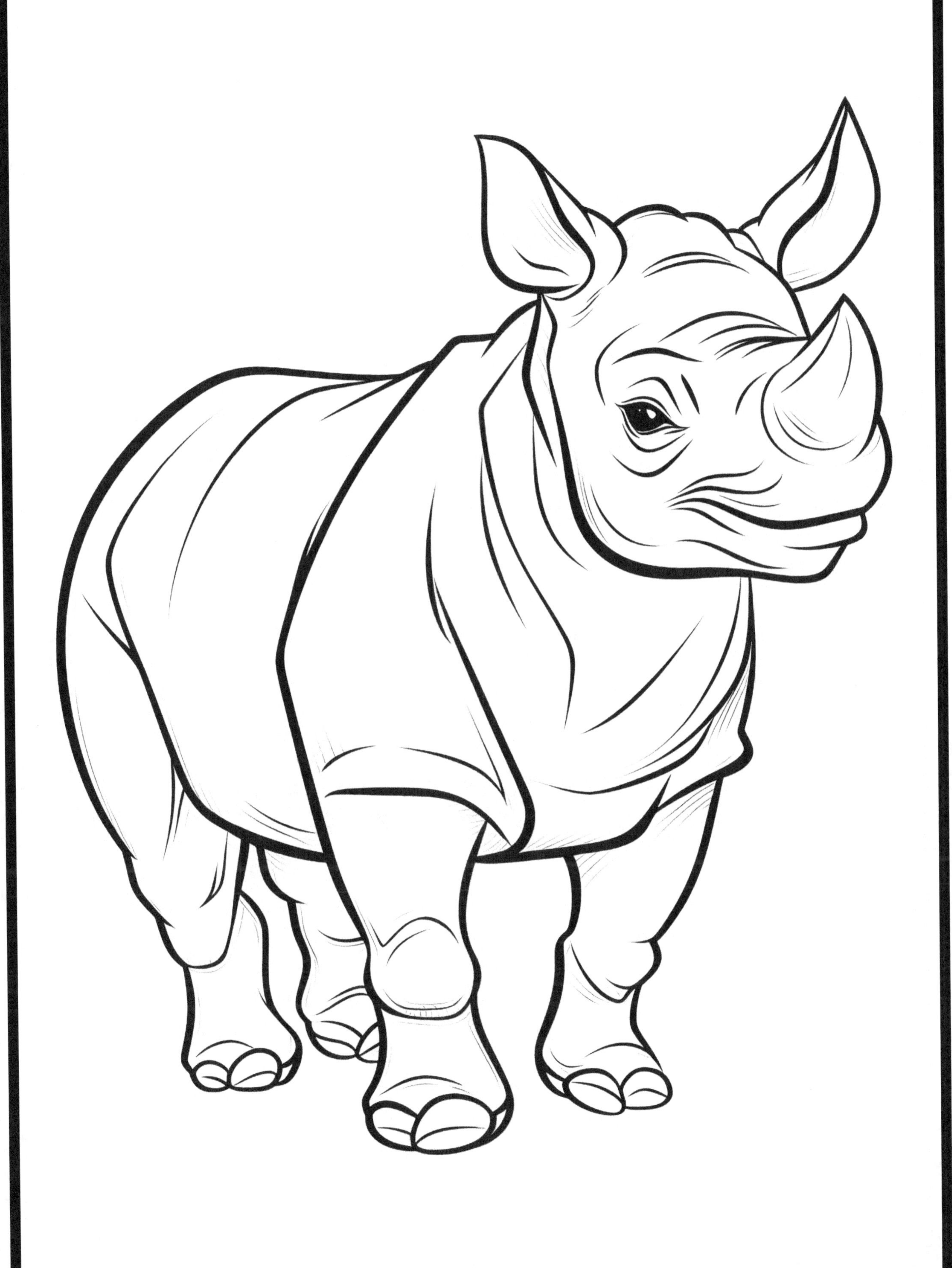

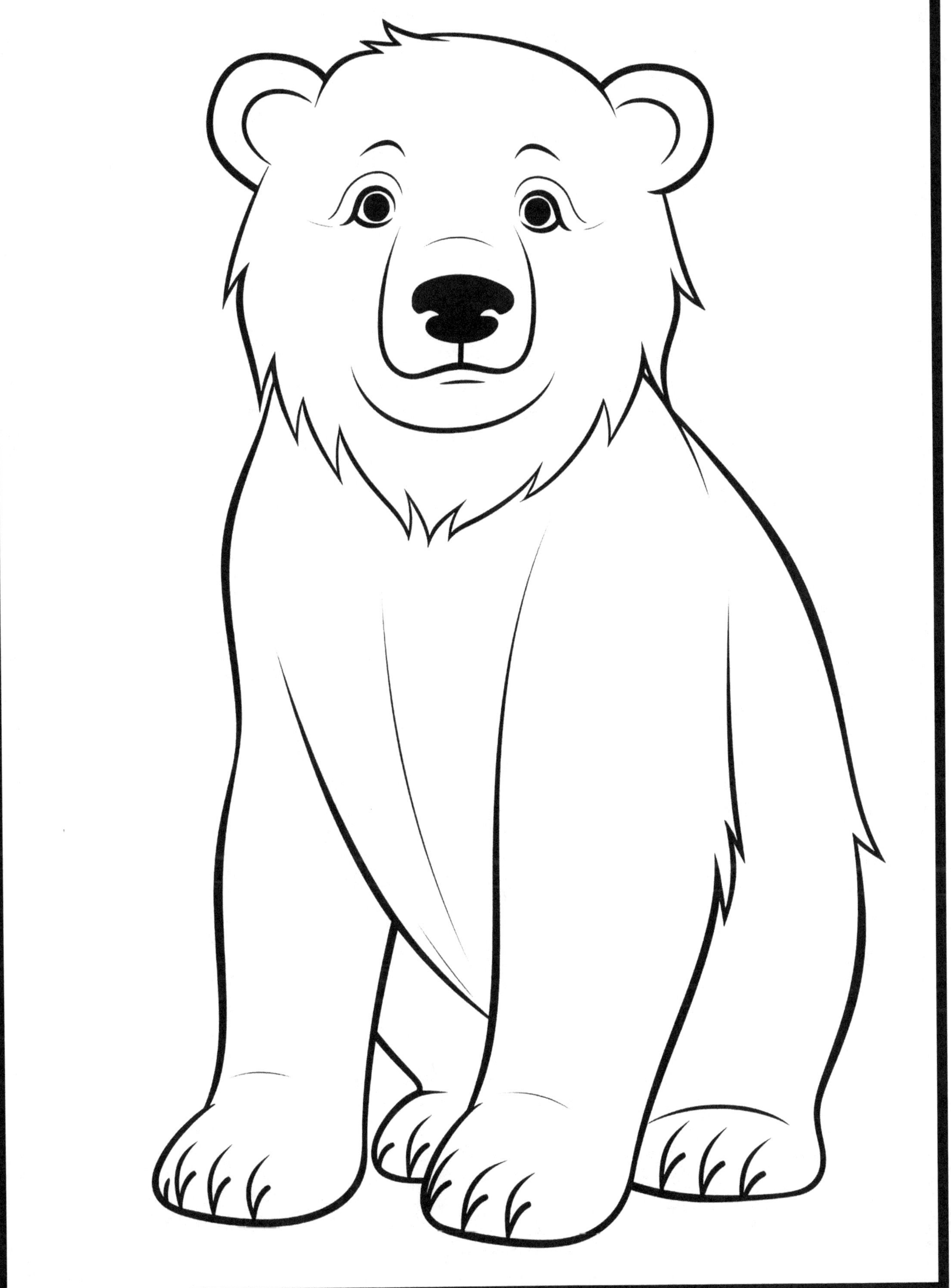

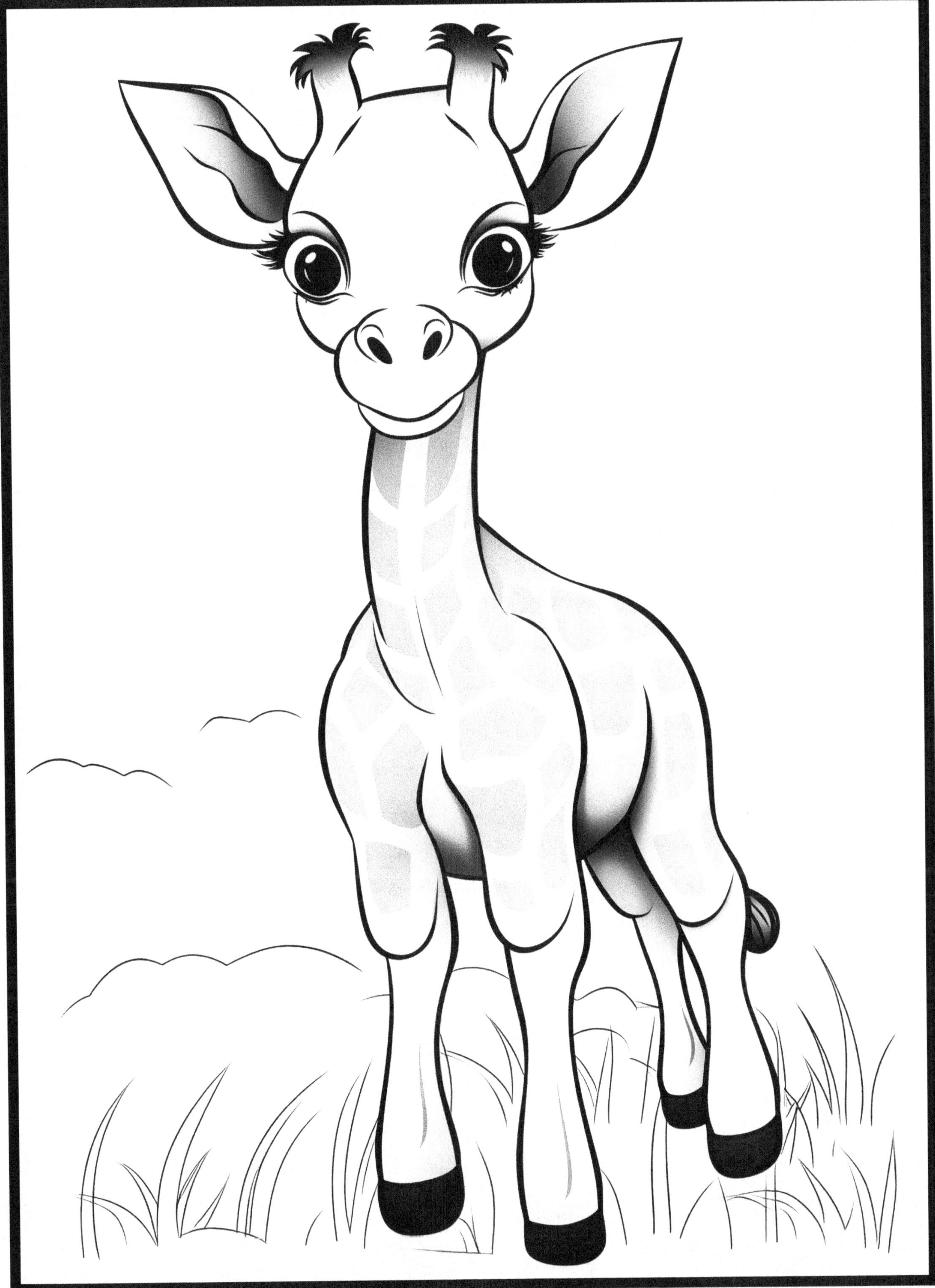

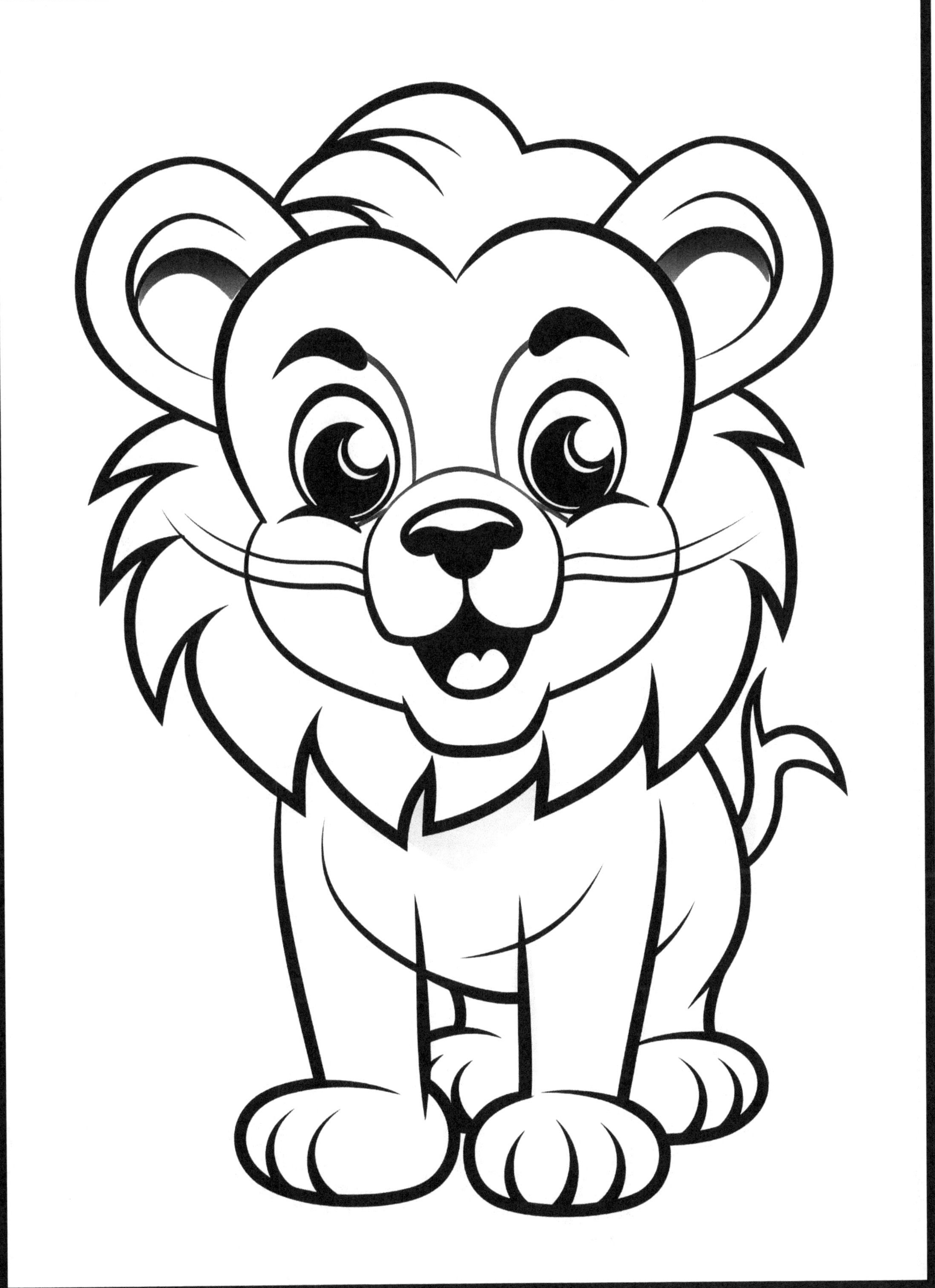

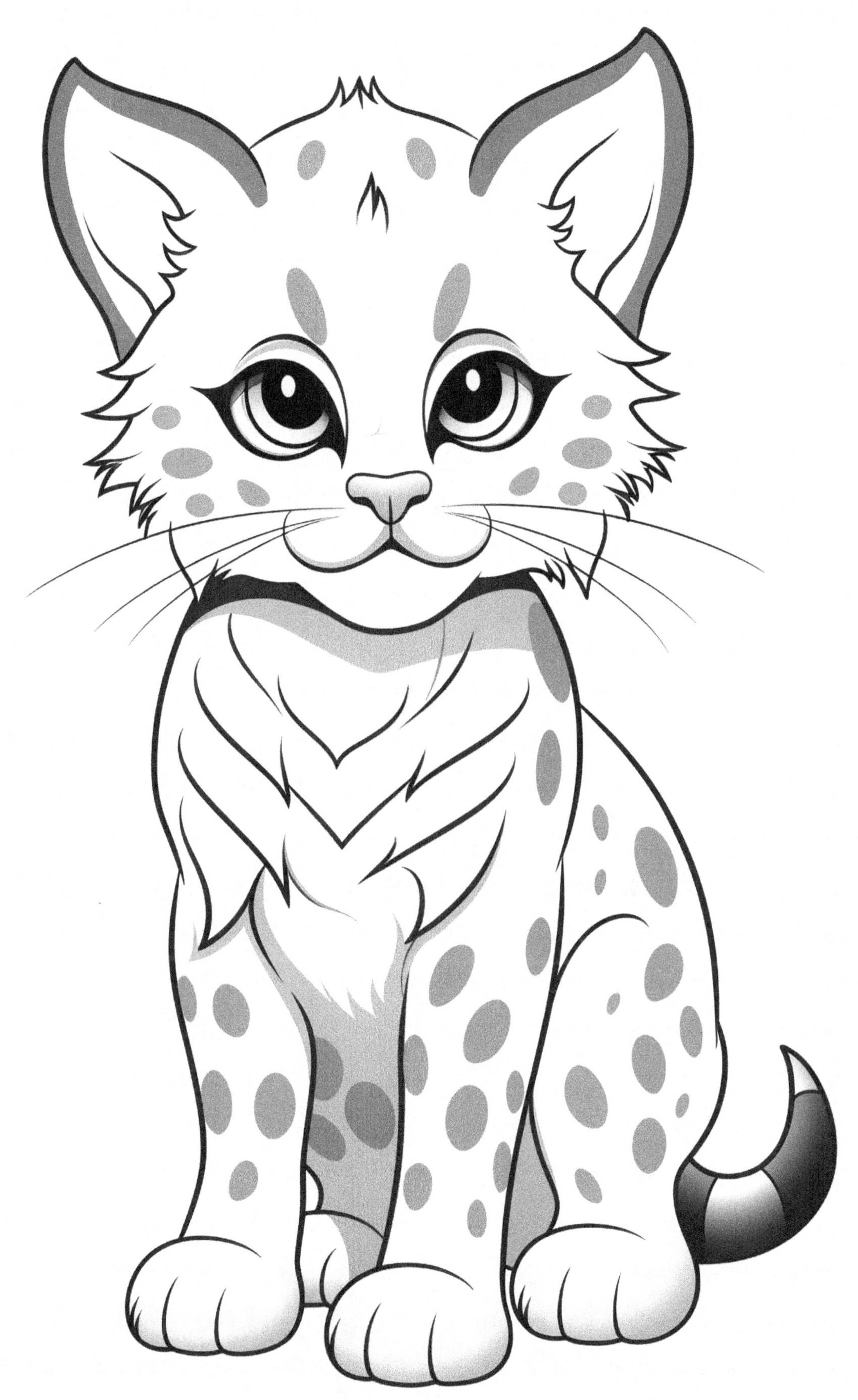

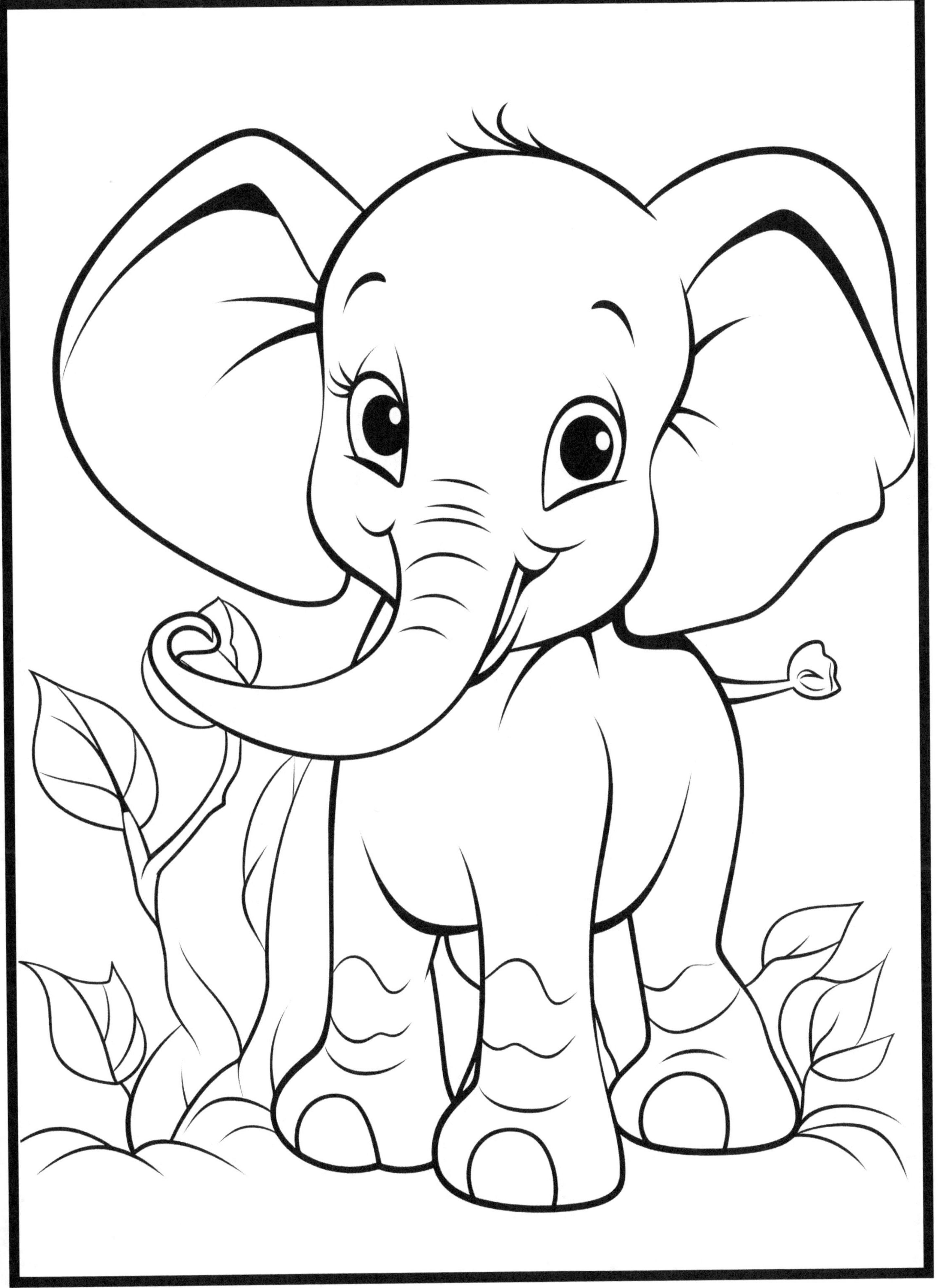

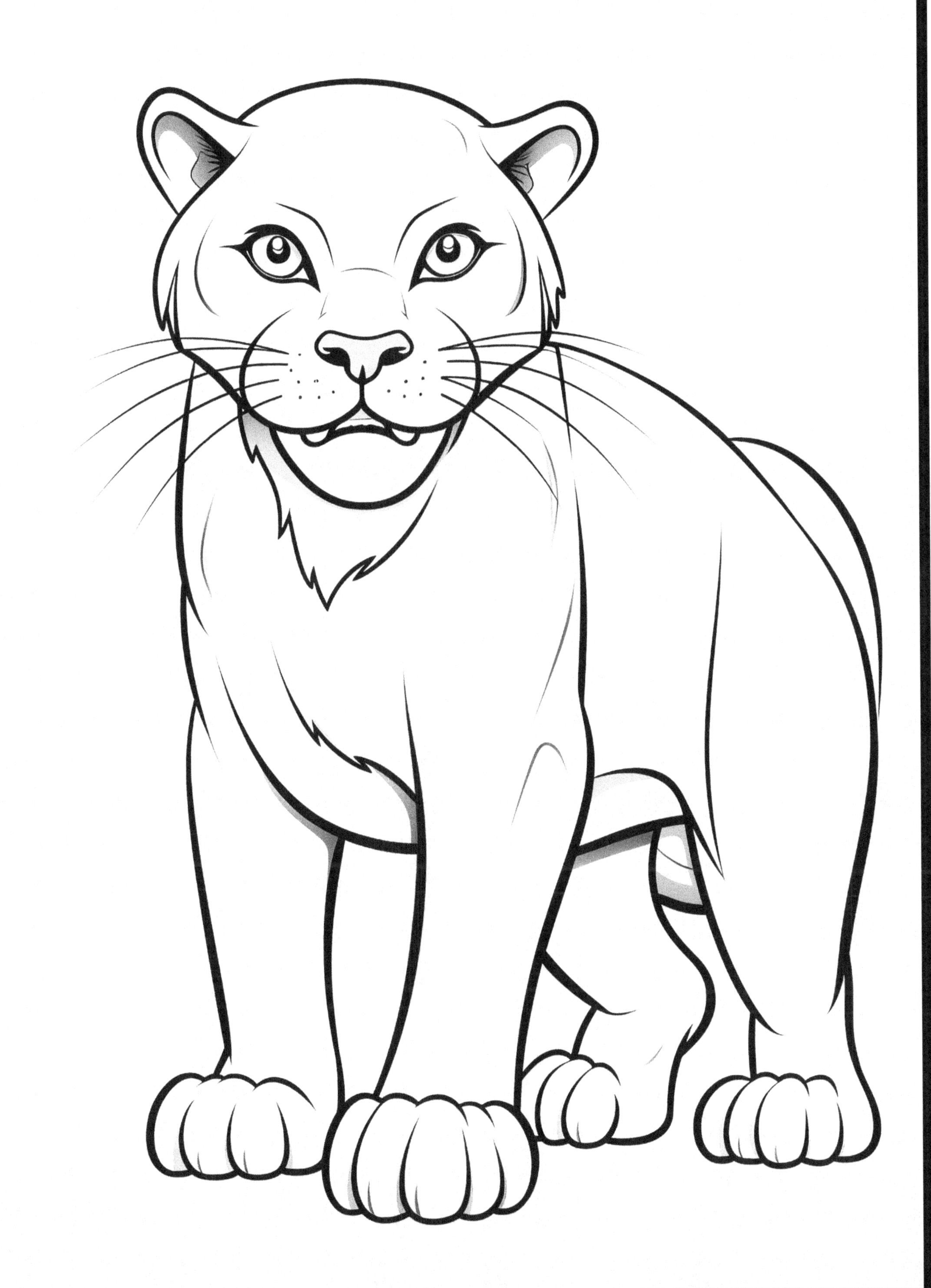

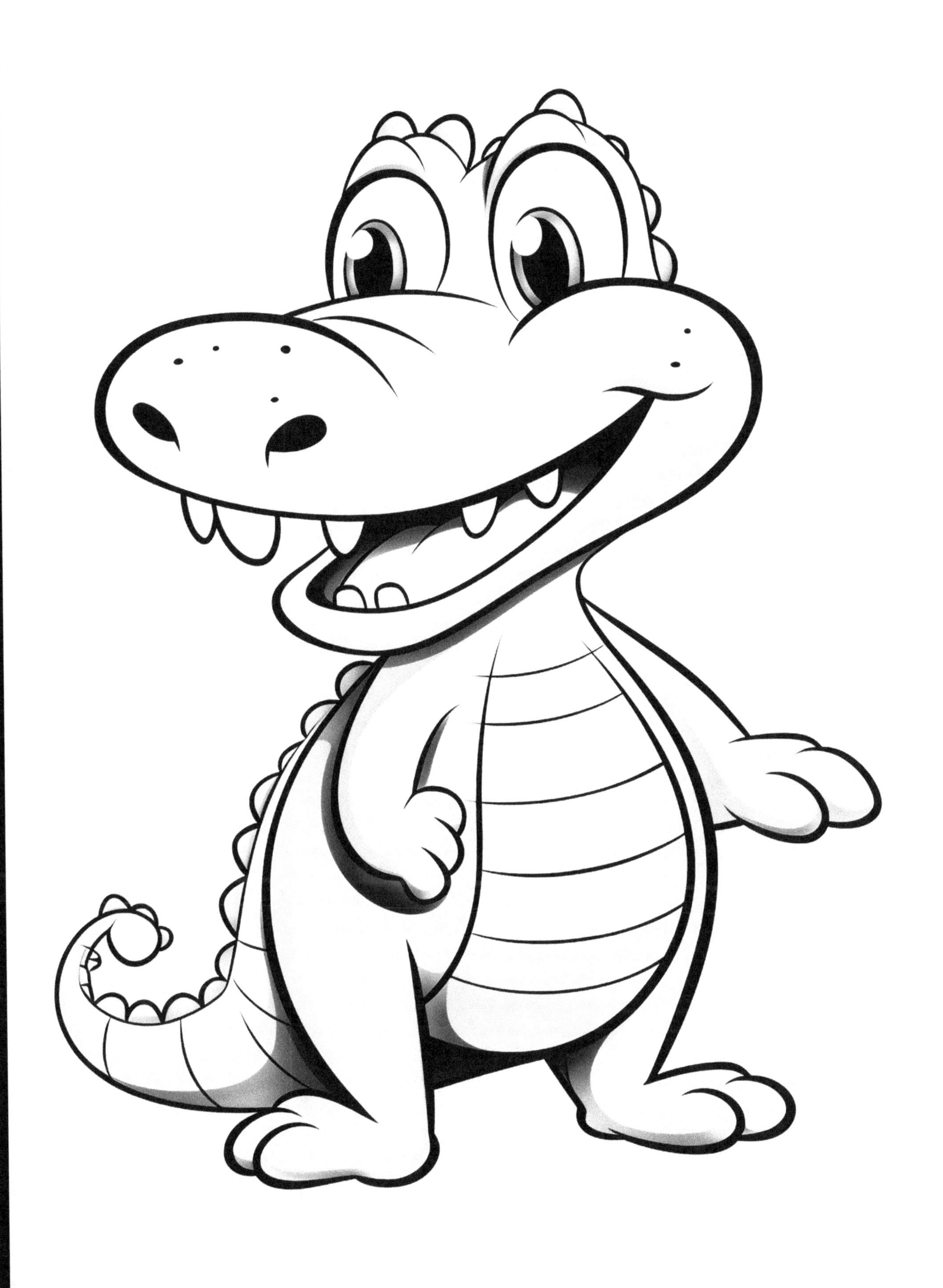

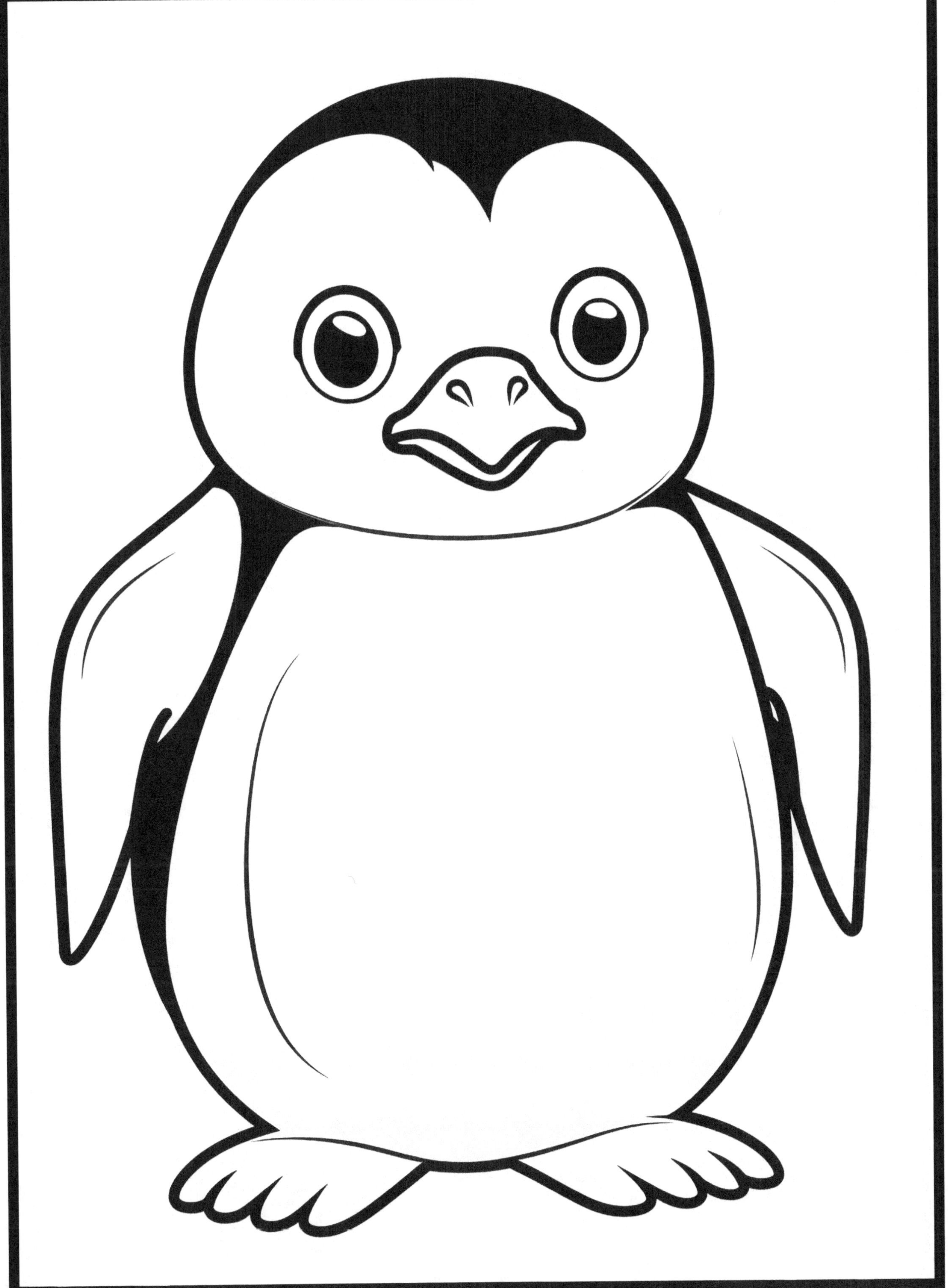

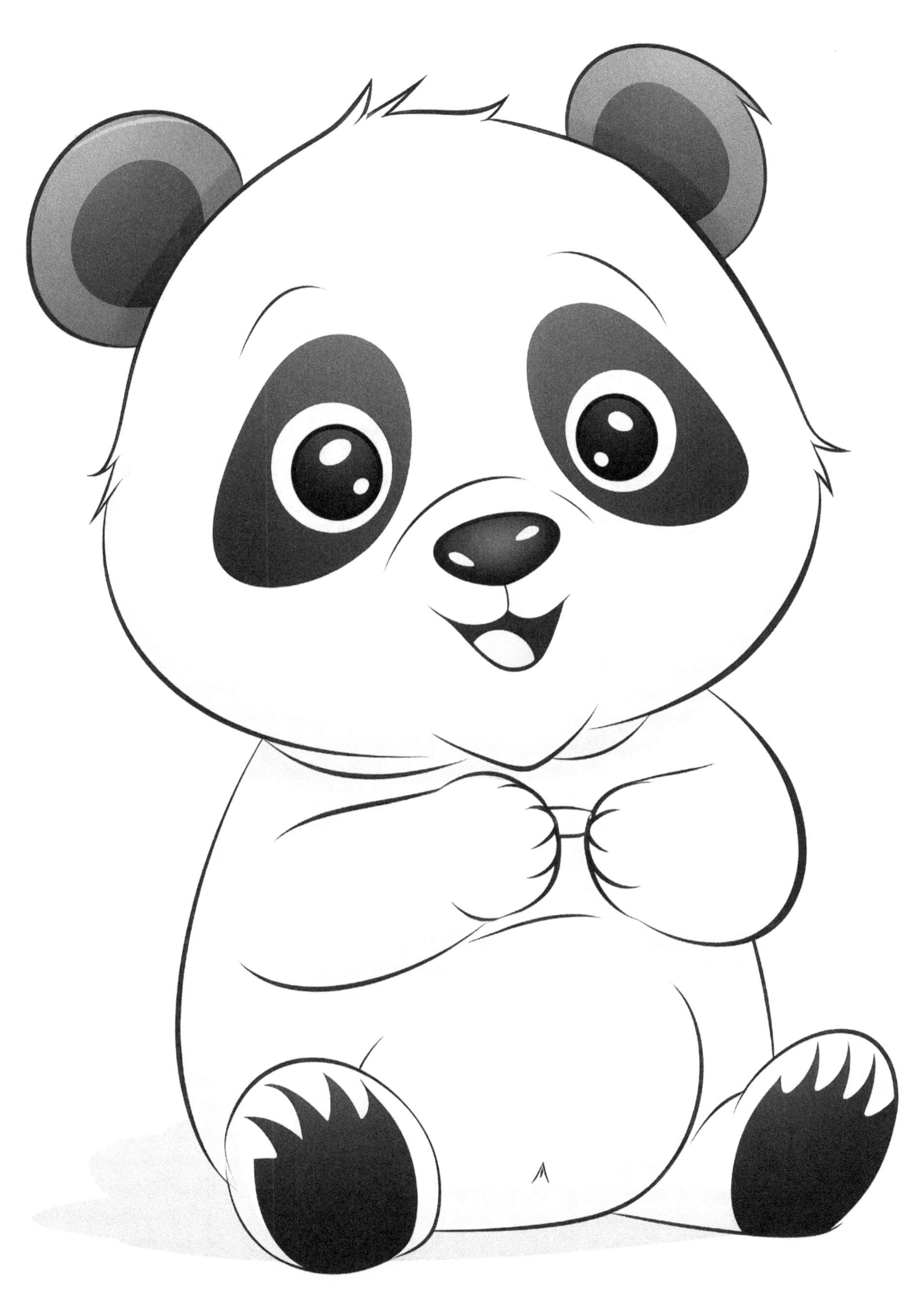

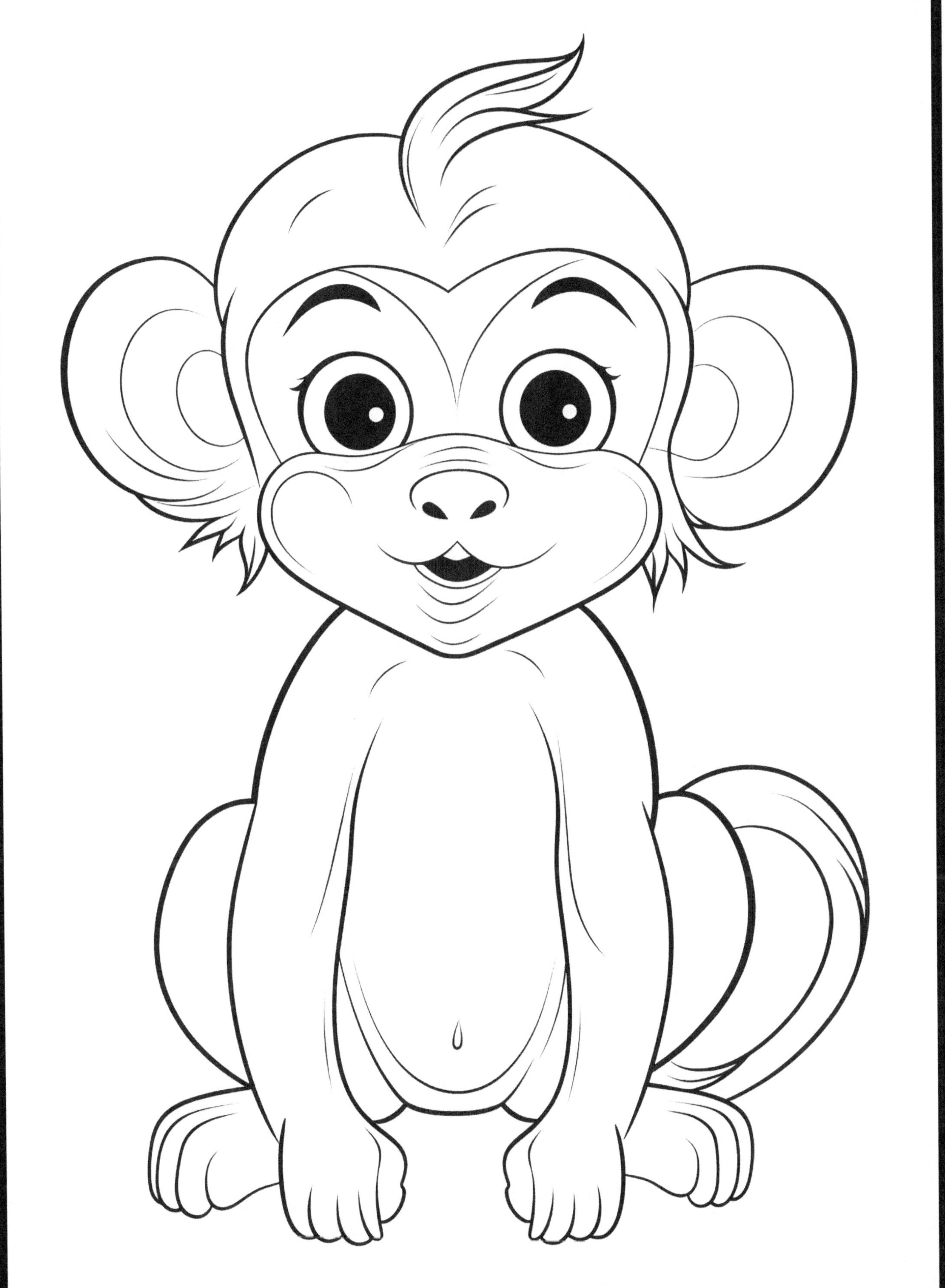

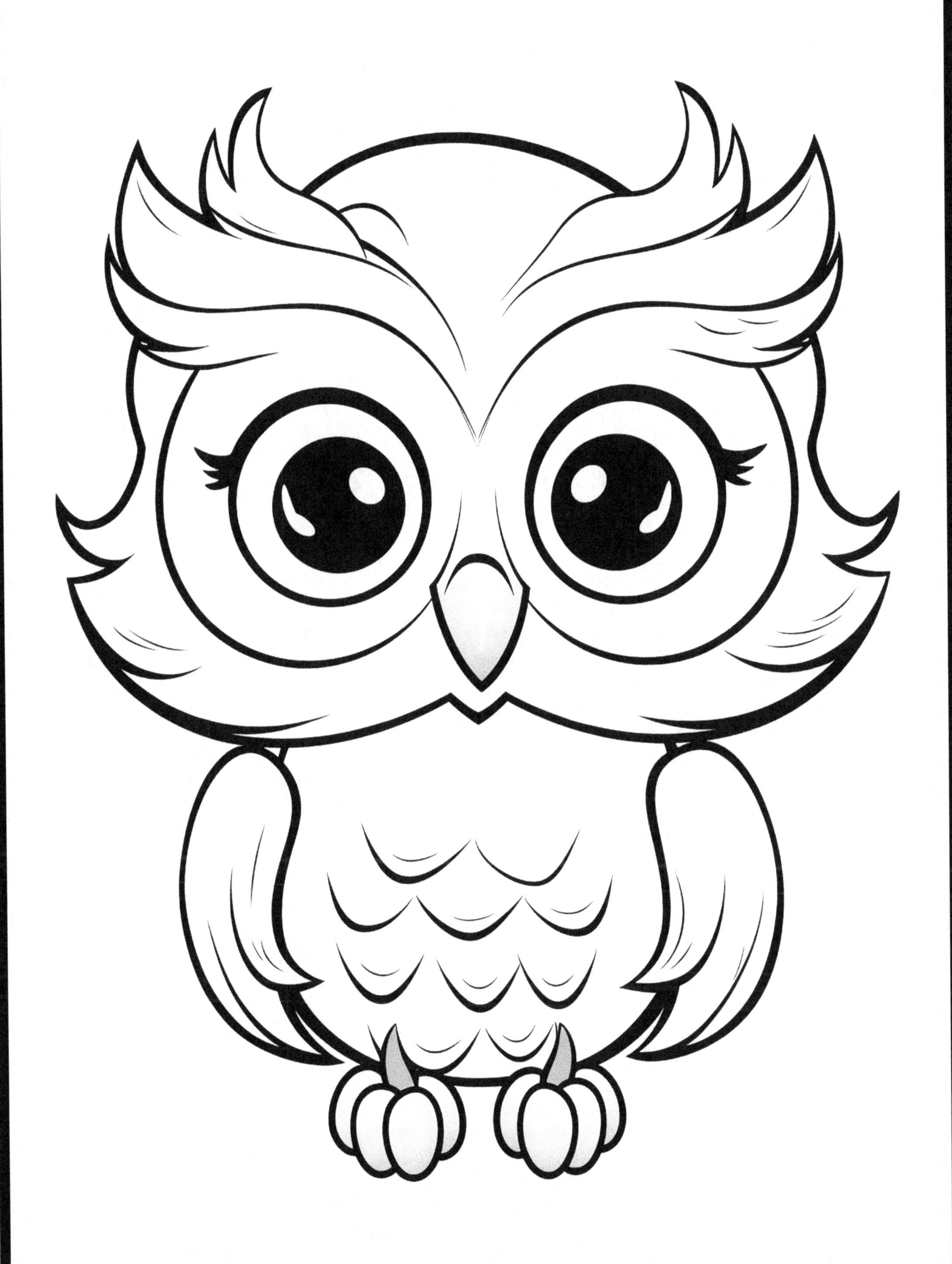

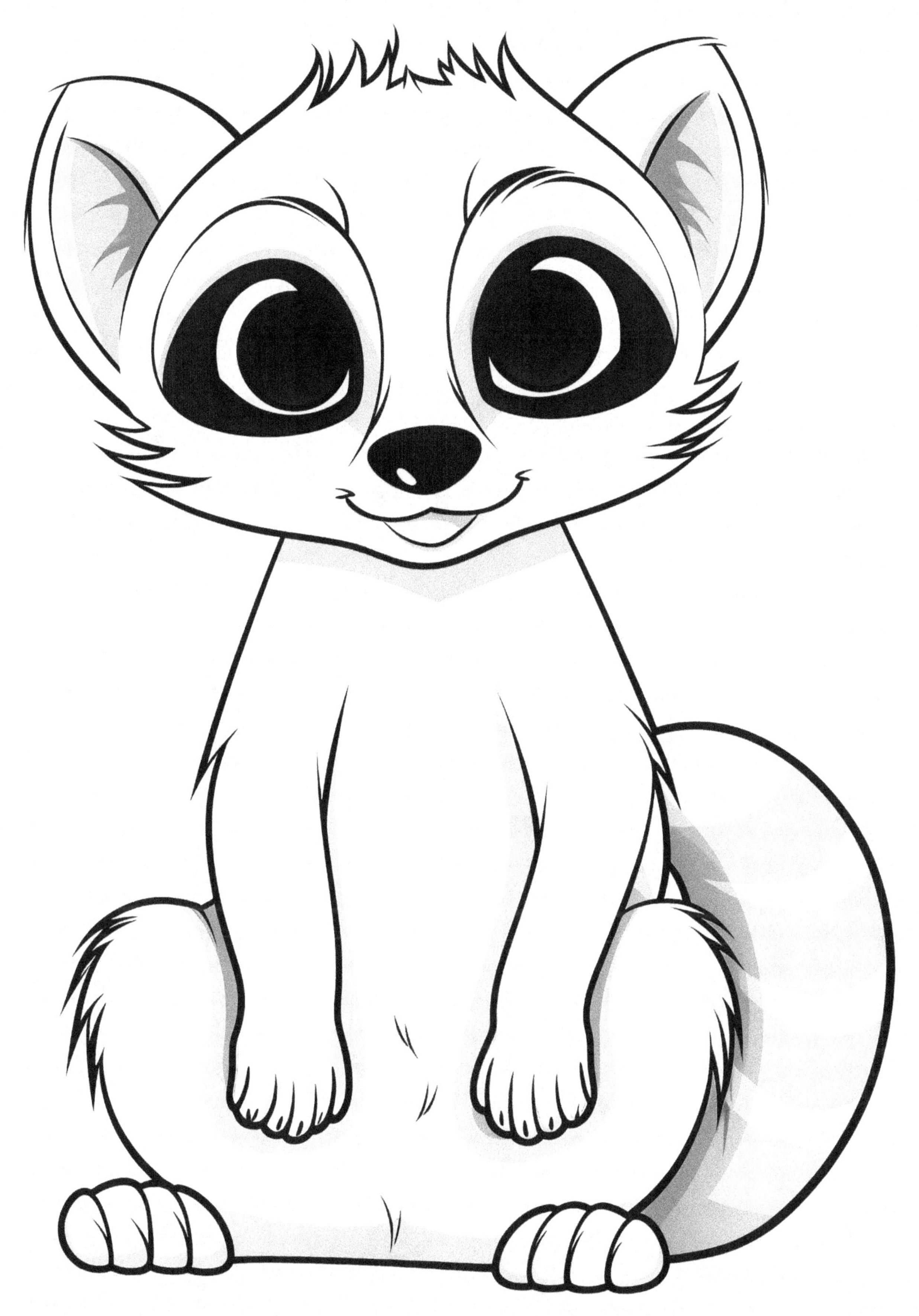

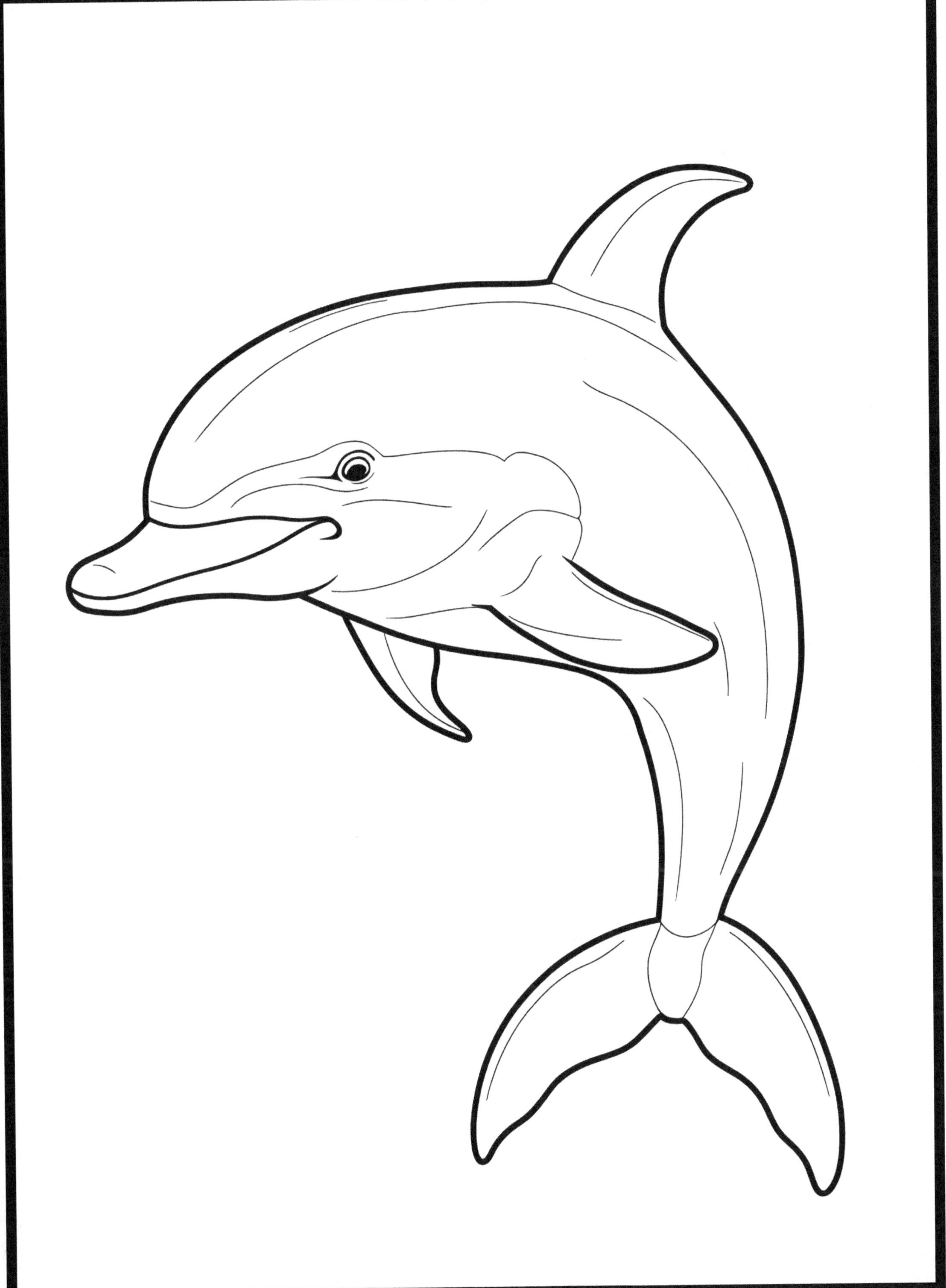

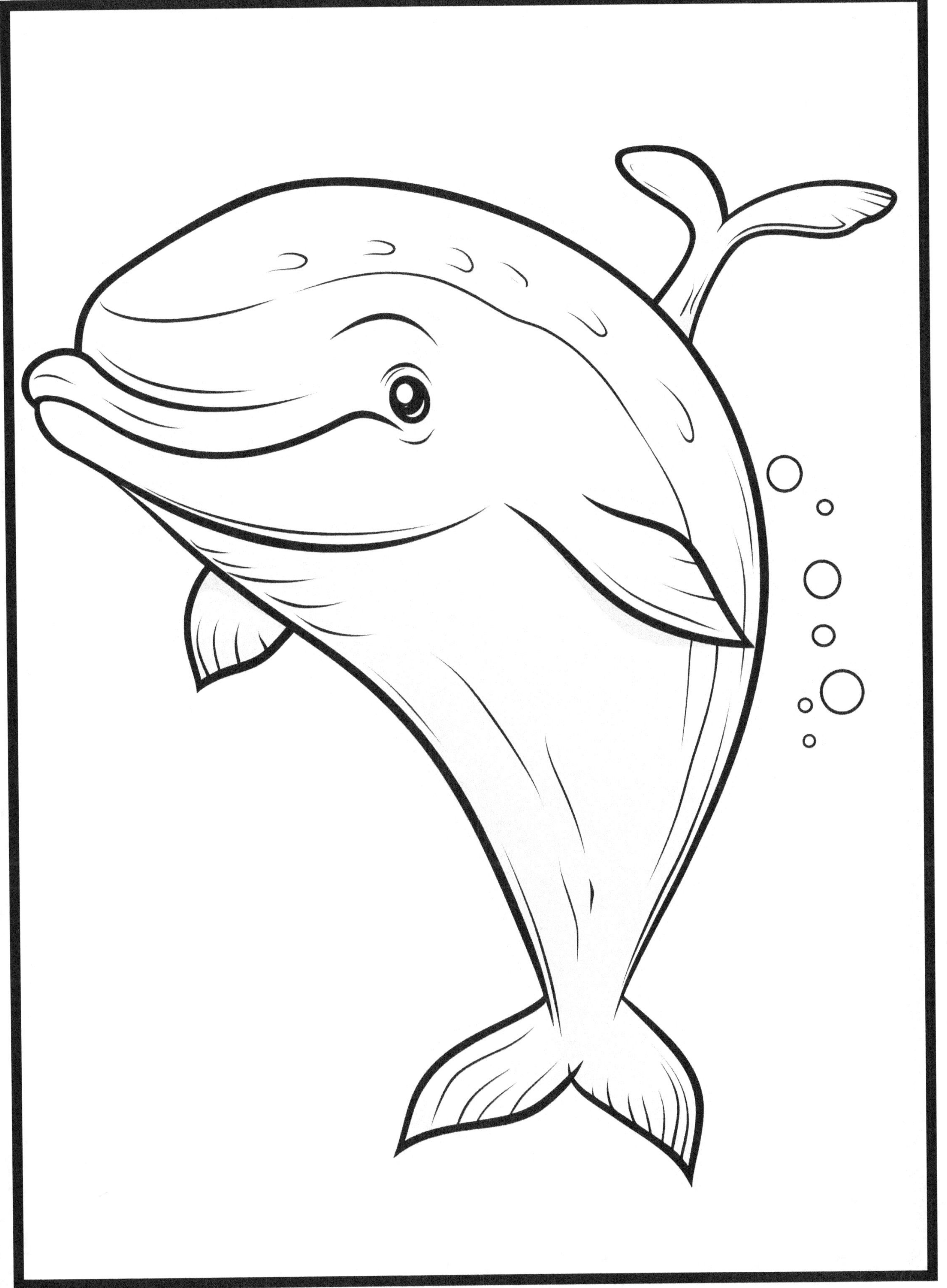

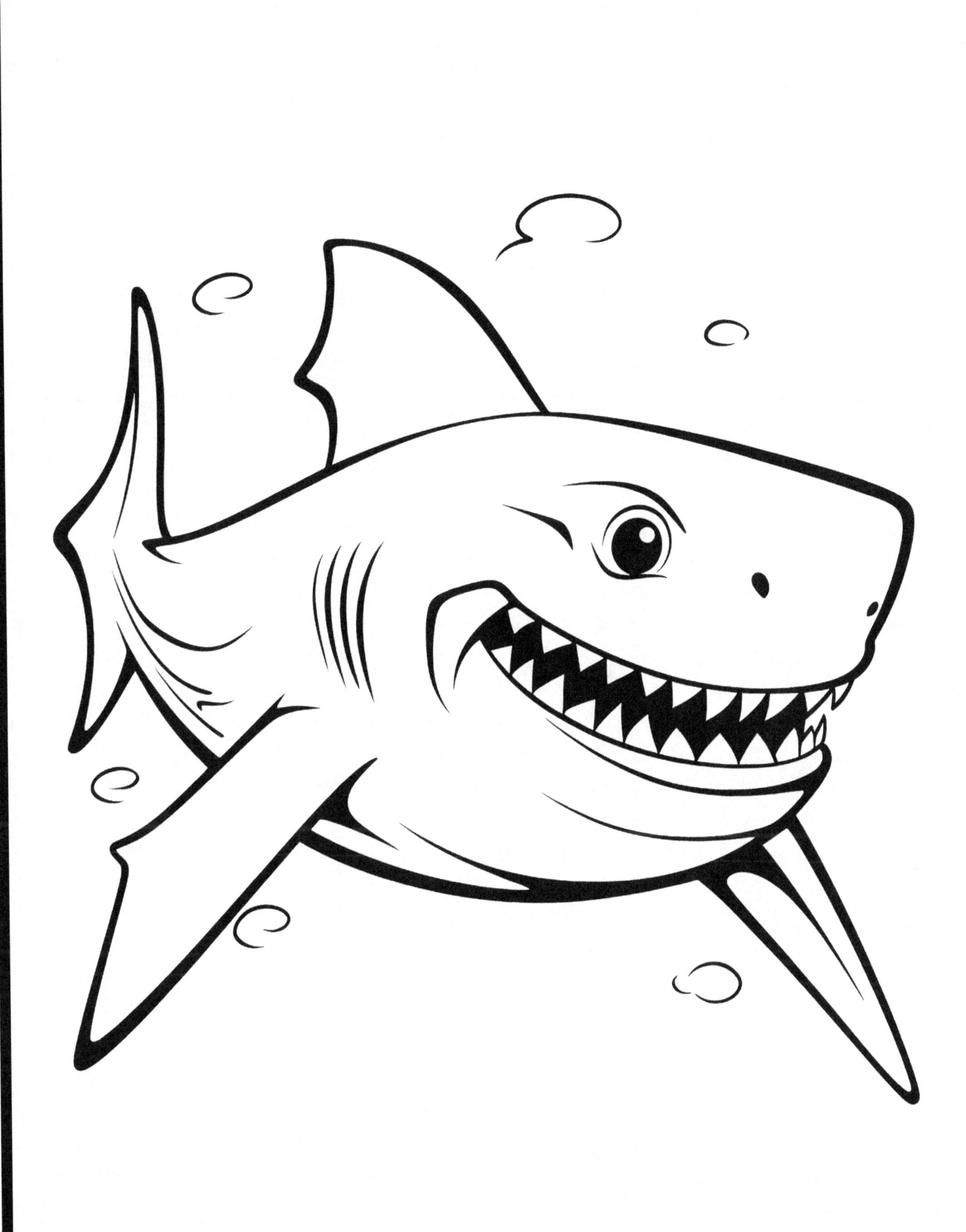

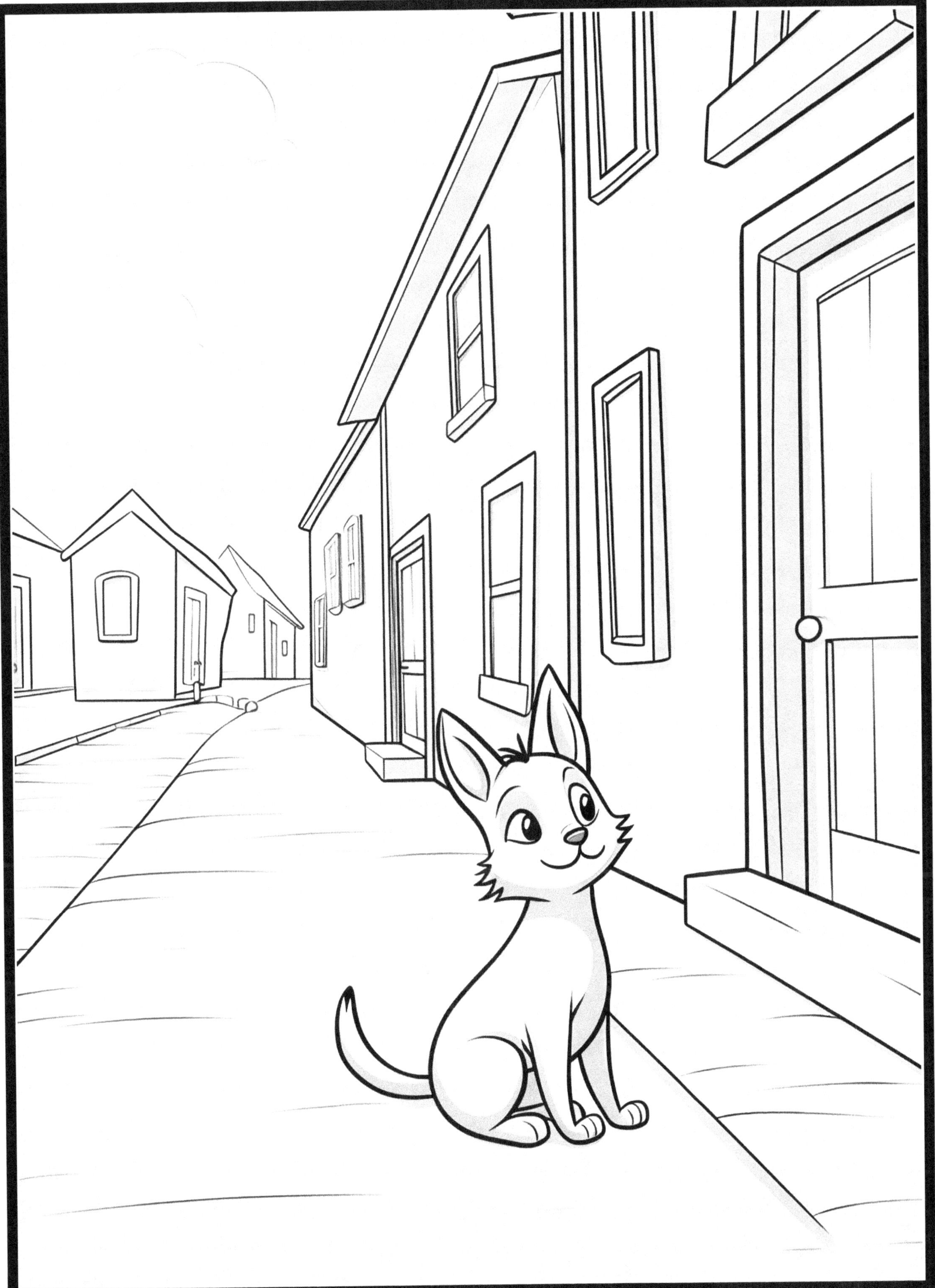

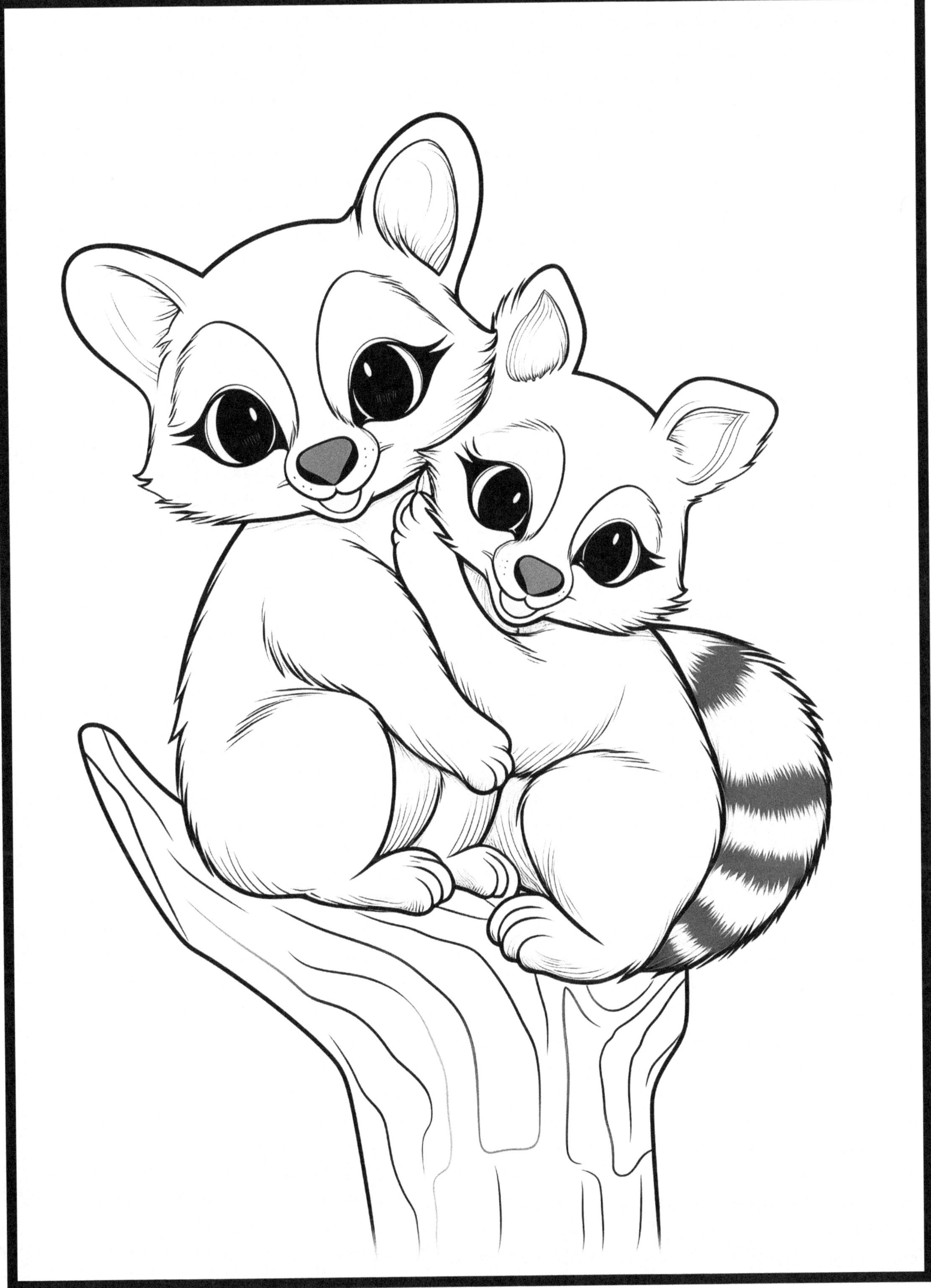

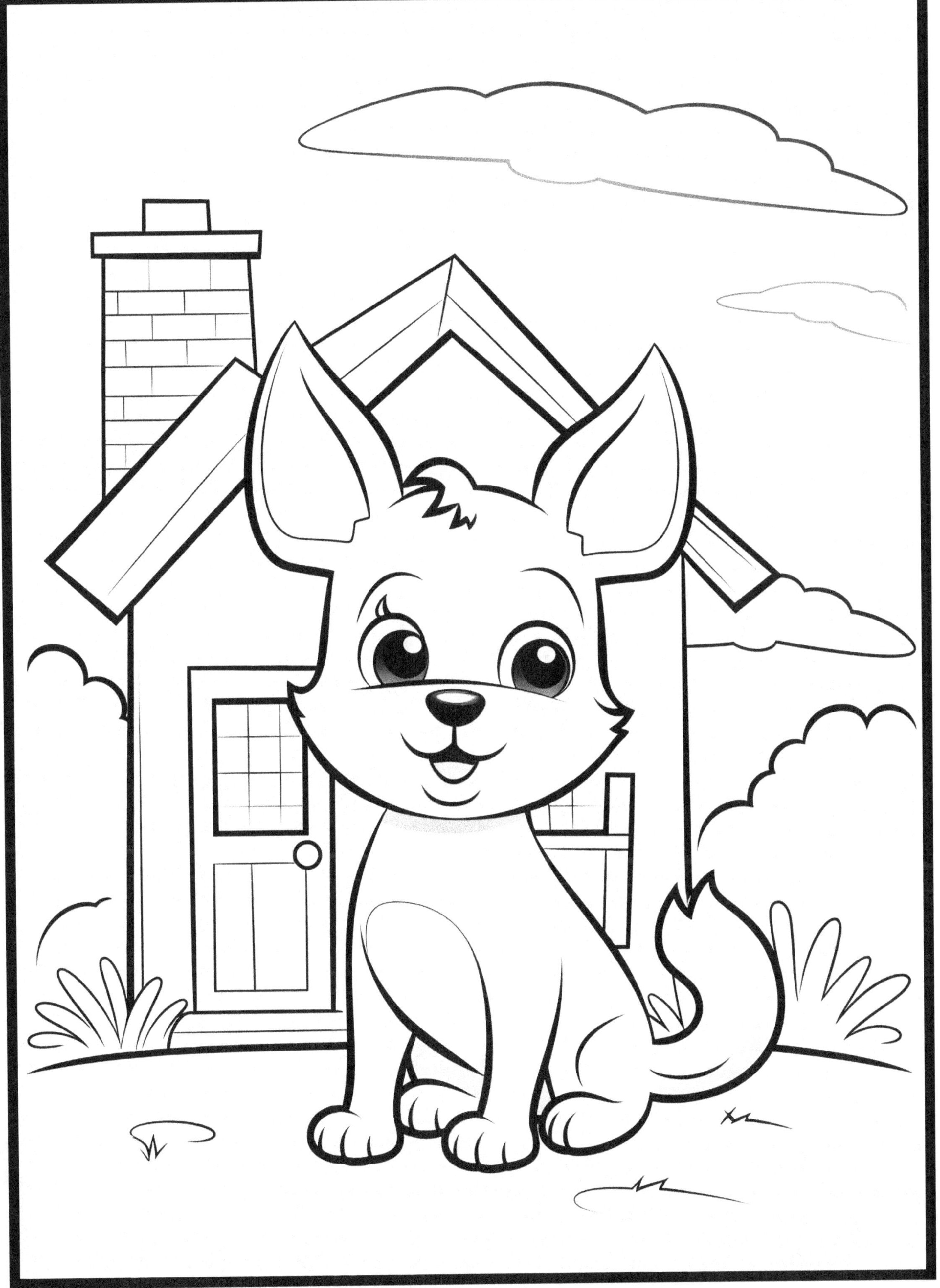

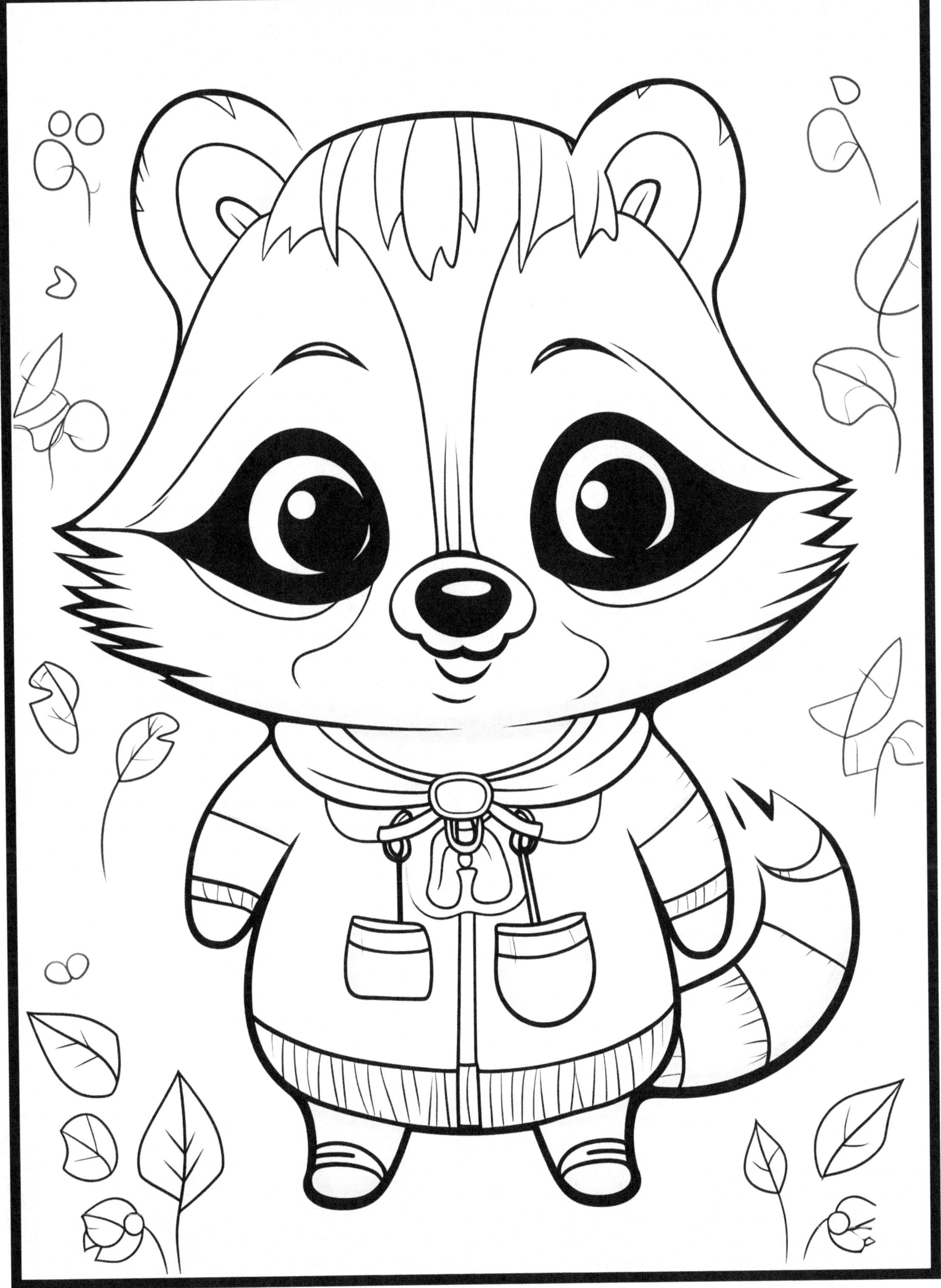

www.ingramcontent.com/pod-product-compliance
Lightning Source LLC
Chambersburg PA
CBHW080917260726
48661CB00009B/3707